Hockey's
Most Wanted

Also by Floyd Conner

Hockey's Most Wanted

The Top 10 Book of Wicked
Slapshots, Bruising Goons,
and Ice Oddities

Floyd Conner

Potomac Books, Inc.
WASHINGTON, D.C.

Library of Congress Cataloging-in-Publication Data

Conner, Floyd, 1951–
    Hockey's most wanted : the top 10 book of
wicked slapshots, bruising goons, and ice
oddities / Floyd Conner.—1st ed.
        p.   cm.
    Includes bibliographical references (p.   )
and index.
    ISBN 1-57488-364-X (pbk.)
    1. Hockey—Miscellanea. I. Title.
GV847 .C617   2002
796.962—dc21

                              200208005

Printed in Canada on acid-free
paper that meets the American National Standards
Institute Z39-48 Standard.

Potomac Books, Inc.
22841 Quicksilver Drive
Dulles, Virginia 20166

First Edition

10 9 8 7 6 5 4 3 2

Contents

Photographs

Introduction

The first hockey game with organized rules was played on March 3, 1875, in Montreal, Canada. The teams were comprised of students from McGill University. Some of the rules differed from the ones used today. There were nine players to a side. The puck was made of wood. There were no nets. In order to score a goal, the puck had to be hit between two sticks. It was illegal to pass the puck or to guard the net.

Hockey's Most Wanted recognizes the sport's most memorable players, outrageous characters, and little-known trivia. The book contains top 10 lists of the worst players, colorful coaches, and the craziest plays in hockey history. The lists feature the unlikeliest heroes, wildest fans, oddest nicknames, outrageous owners, biggest goons, most embarrassing moments, and the strangest things to occur in a hockey rink.

Some things that have happened in hockey border on the unbelievable. Ottawa goaltender Fred Chittick refused to play in the 1898 Stanley Cup playoffs because he was not given enough complimentary tickets. Another Ottawa player, Cy Denneny, led the National Hockey League (NHL) in scoring in 1924 despite having only one assist all season. Montreal's Maurice "the Rocket" Richard led the NHL in goals scored five times but never led the league in scoring. Chicago goaltender Al Rollins won the NHL's Most Valuable Player Award in 1954 despite having a 12-47-7 record. Tom Martin, a player for the Seattle Breakers, was once traded for a bus.

Hockey players have some of the most unusual nicknames in sports. Hall of Fame goaltender Georges Vezina was known as the Chicoutimi Cucumber. Center Max Bentley's nickname was the Dipsy Doodle Dandy from Delisle. The hockey-playing dentist Bill Carson was called the Stratford Teethpuller. Frank Finnigan's unusual nickname was the Slumbering Romeo. Defenseman Jim Hargreaves was given the moniker of Cement Head.

The sport has had its share of colorful characters. Goalie Gilles Gratton streaked in practice and believed he had been reincarnated many times. Owner Eddie Shore made his players tap-dance in hotel lobbies and practice in darkened rinks. Center Mike "Shaky" Walton once did a television interview while wearing only a small patch of shaving cream. All Star left wing Brendan Shanahan had a false bio printed in his team's media guide in which he claimed to make his movie debut in *Forrest Gump*.

Not every player can be Wayne Gretzky. New York Rangers goaltender Steve Buzinski once accidentally threw the puck into his own net and was so inept that he was given the nickname the Puck Goesinski. Another Rangers goalie, Tubby McAuley, set a record for futility by allowing 15 goals in a game. Don Spring played in 259 NHL games and scored only one goal. It took Larry Melnyk five seasons to score his first NHL goal.

No hockey team would be complete without a goon. Baldy Spittal was such a dirty player that he was chased from an arena by fans. In 1927, Boston's Billy Coutu was banned from the NHL for life for savagely attacking an official. Montreal's Sprague Cleghorn injured three Ottawa players in one game. Randy Holt of the Los Angeles Kings set a record by being assessed 67 penalty minutes in one game, an incredible feat considering the game lasted only 60 minutes. Dave "the Hammer" Schultz, one of Philadelphia's notorious Broad Street Bullies, set the single season record for bad behavior with 472 penalty minutes during the 1974–1975 season.

This book introduces you to nearly 700 of hockey's most wanted players, owners, and fans. Their offenses range from inept play to outrageous behavior. Be on the lookout for these individuals.

The First Period

B illy Reay, a center with the Montreal Canadiens in the 1940s, was the first player to raise his stick to celebrate scoring a goal. In 1955, another Montreal center, Jean Beliveau, was the first hockey player to be featured on the cover of *Sports Illustrated*. Boston's Bobby Orr was the first defenseman to score more than 100 points in a season. Here are 10 more notable hockey firsts.

1. **JAMES CREIGHTON**

The first organized hockey game took place on March 3, 1875, at the Victoria Rink in Montreal. A team captained by a McGill University student named James Creighton won by the score of 2 to 1. There were nine players to a side, three more than there are in the modern game. Goals were scored by hitting the puck between two sticks placed eight feet apart. Nets were not used until many years later. Players were not allowed to pass the puck forward or protect their goal. The game was already violent, and several of the female spectators fled in horror.

2. AMATEUR HOCKEY ASSOCIATION OF CANADA

The first hockey league, the Amateur Hockey Association of Canada, was established in 1887. The teams were composed entirely of amateur players. The International League, hockey's first professional league, was organized in 1905.

3. DAVE RITCHIE

The first goal in the National Hockey League was scored by Montreal Wanderers defenseman Dave Ritchie in a 10-9 victory over Toronto on December 19, 1917. Ritchie scored only 15 goals during his six-year NHL career.

4. FRANK NIGHBOR

In 1924, Frank Nighbor, a center with the Ottawa Senators, was the first recipient of the Hart Memorial Trophy, presented annually to the National Hockey League's Most Valuable Player. Nighbor scored 10 goals and had three assists in 20 games, but was given the award for his excellent all-around play. The next season Nighbor was the first Lady Byng Memorial Trophy winner in recognition of his outstanding sportsmanship.

5. CLINT BENEDICT

On February 20, 1930, Clint Benedict of the Montreal Maroons became the first goaltender to wear a mask. Benedict wore the leather mask to protect a broken nose. The mask had a big nosepiece and obstructed the goalie's vision. The primitive mask also kept coming loose. Benedict reinjured his nose later that season and retired from hockey.

6. MAURICE RICHARD

Maurice Richard of the Montreal Canadiens was the first NHL player to score 50 goals in a season. Richard scored 50 goals in 50 games during the 1944–1945 season. That same year Richard's Montreal teammate, Elmer Lach, became the first player to reach 50 assists during a season.

7. EMILE FRANCIS

Emile "the Cat" Francis was the first goalie to wear a glove. The 22-year-old goaltender first wore the glove, similar to a baseball mitt, in 1948. The NHL approved the new piece of equipment and by the end of the season most of the league's goaltenders wore gloves to help them catch the puck.

8. JACQUES PLANTE

The first goaltender to wear a mask on a continuous basis was Jacques Plante of the Montreal Canadiens. On November 1, 1959, Plante suffered a seven-stitch cut when he was struck in the face by a hard shot by Andy Bathgate of the New York Rangers. Plante, who had suffered from broken noses, two fractured cheekbones, a broken jaw, and more than 200 stitches in his face during his career, had a fiberglass mask made for protection. At first, Montreal coach Toe Blake did not want his star goaltender to wear the mask, fearing that it might limit his vision. He changed his mind when the Canadiens, with Plante in the net, went on an 18-game unbeaten streak. Soon other goalies began wearing masks, although it would be another 15 years before the last maskless goaltender.

9. GARRY MONAHAN

The first National Hockey League draft occurred in 1963. The first player selected was 16-year-old Garry Monahan, who was picked by the Montreal Canadiens. The left winger scored 116 goals during his NHL career from 1967 to 1979.

10. PHIL ESPOSITO

The first player to score 100 points in a season was Boston Bruins center Phil Esposito. During the 1968–1969 season, Esposito had 49 goals and 77 assists for a total of 126 points.

Rules of the Game

Over the years, hockey rules have changed. In the early days of hockey, the game was divided into two 30-minute halves instead of three 20-minute periods. There was a seventh player called the "rover." During the 1920s, referees rang bells to signal penalties, unlike today's officials who blow whistles.

1. THE McGILL RULES

Hockey's first rules were written by three McGill University students in 1877. There were 9 players to a side. Previously, any number of players could participate. In some games, there were as many as 40 players on a team. A lacrosse ball was used until it was realized that a wooden puck traveled better across the ice. The game was over when one of the teams scored three goals.

2. FRED WAGHORNE

The faceoff was originated by referee Fred Waghorne in 1900. Prior to the creation of the faceoff, a procedure known as the "bully" was used to determine which team gained possession. In a bully, one player from each team would click their sticks three times before hitting the puck.

3. CORNWALL

At the turn of the twentieth century, a goal judge made the call on whether or not a goal was scored. That changed after a dispute in Ontario, Canada, between teams from Cornwall and Morrisburg. The game was won by Morrisburg on a disputed goal. Fans from Cornwall hired an attorney and 200 of them signed an affidavit that the goal was no good. In response, 200 fans from Morrisburg signed an affidavit that the goal did cross the goal line. As a result of the controversy, the referee, and not the goal judge, was given the authority to decide whether or not a goal was scored.

4. FLOPPING

On January 19, 1918, the NHL adopted a rule that allowed goaltenders to fall to their knees to make a save. Prior to the rule change, a goalie was assessed a minor penalty and fined two dollars for "flopping." Goalie Clint Benedict perfected an act in which he pretended to lose his balance to stop the puck.

5. SPARE GOALTENDER

In the early years of the NHL, some teams carried only one goaltender on their rosters. In 1928, the league passed a rule that, in the case of a goalie being injured, allowed the opposing team to loan them their spare goalie. The team was to be paid $200 per game for his services. Not surprisingly, teams were reluctant to loan their goaltender and the rule was eventually rescinded.

6. CHARLES ADAMS

Before the icing rule was adopted, teams routinely shot the puck the length of the ice to relieve pressure in their zone. In one game, played on January 3, 1932, the

Boston Bruins iced the puck an incredible 87 times. Bruins owner Charles Adams, realizing that the practice resulted in low-scoring dull games, proposed the first icing rule in 1932. The rule stated that a faceoff would occur in the defending team's zone any time the puck was intentionally shot to the other end to relieve pressure. The rule was not adopted for another five seasons.

7. JEAN BELIVEAU

The great Montreal Canadien teams of the 1950s were deadly with their power plays. At the time, an opposing player had to remain in the penalty box for the duration of the penalty. On November 5, 1955, Montreal's Jean Beliveau scored a hat trick in 44 seconds during a power play against Boston. The next season, the rule was changed so that a player would leave the penalty box if a goal was scored during a power play.

8. RON STACKHOUSE

Roger Neilson was a coach known for his broad interpretation of the rules. While a junior hockey coach in Peterborough, Ontario, Neilson replaced his goalie with rugged defenseman Ron Stackhouse on penalty shots. When the shooter skated in, Stackhouse came out and checked him before he could get off the shot. Neilson pointed out correctly that there was no rule that stopped the goalie from checking the shooter. The rule was soon changed.

9. ROGER NEILSON

Roger Neilson also created an ingenious way to stop open net goals. When he would pull his goaltender at the end of the game to add another attacker, Neilson

Frank Prazak/Hockey Hall of Fame

Jean Beliveau of the Montreal Canadiens chases a puck into
the corner as the Toronto Maple Leafs' goaltender keeps a
close eye on the quick-strike scorer.

told the goalie to break his stick in half and lay the
pieces in front of the goal in an attempt to deflect any
shots shot down the ice by the other team. Once again,
a rule was modified by a Roger Neilson play.

10. STAN MIKITA

Chicago Black Hawks right winger Stan Mikita scored
541 goals during his NHL career that lasted from 1958

to 1980. Early in his career, Mikita used a curved stick called the "banana blade." The extreme curvature of the stick caused the flight of his shots to behave erratically, making them more difficult to stop. A rule was adopted that limited the curve of a stick to one-half inch.

Rocket and the Golden Jet

Sometimes a player is better known by his nickname than by his real name. King Clancy's real name was Francis. Garnet Bailey was known to hockey fans as Ace. The following are some of hockey's most recognizable nicknames.

1. ROCKET

Maurice Richard was a rookie with Montreal in 1942. When the swift skating Richard sped by, teammate Ray Getliffe said, "Look out, here comes the rocket!" "Rocket" Richard went on to become one of hockey's most dynamic stars.

2. THE GOLDEN JET

Bobby Hull was hockey's golden boy during the 1960s. Hull's curly blond hair only enhanced his golden image. One of the fastest skaters of his time, the Golden Jet was the first NHL player to score more than 50 goals in a season.

3. BOOM BOOM

Bernie Geoffrion had one of the best and loudest slap shots in hockey. Geoffrion was given the name Boom

Boom because of the sound it made when he hit it and when the puck struck the boards. Boom Boom found the net 393 times during his career, primarily spent with the Montreal Canadiens.

4. **MR. ZERO**

Frank Brimsek had a sensational rookie season with the Boston Bruins in 1938. The goaltender was given the nickname Mr. Zero after recording six shutouts in his first eight games. Brimsek had 40 shutouts during his Hall of Fame career. Brimsek preferred the nickname to his other monikers, "the Minnesota Icicle" and "Frigid Frankie."

5. **SUDDEN DEATH**

Mel Hill was given the nickname Sudden Death because of his clutch play in the 1939 Stanley Cup final between Boston and New York. The Bruins' right winger won three of the games with overtime goals.

6. **THE GREAT ONE**

If ever a hockey player deserved the nickname of the Great One, it was Wayne Gretzky. The NHL's all-time leading scorer, Gretzky led the Edmonton Oilers to four Stanley Cup titles. Gretzky is considered by most experts the greatest player in hockey history.

7. **THE OLD LAMPLIGHTER**

Hector "Toe" Blake was called the Old Lamplighter because of his ability to score goals. Blake lit the goal light 235 times during his NHL career. After he retired as a player, Blake coached the Montreal Canadiens to eight Stanley Cup championships.

8. OLD POISON

Center Nels Stewart was nicknamed Old Poison because of his deadly shot. Stewart had such contempt for the goaltenders that he sometimes spit tobacco juice in their eyes when he took a shot near the net. When Stewart retired in 1940, his 324 goals was an NHL record.

9. THE CHINA WALL

Goaltender Johnny Bower was called the China Wall because it was difficult to get a puck past him. Bower won 250 games and registered 37 shutouts during his NHL career.

10. THE POCKET ROCKET

Henri Richard was Maurice "the Rocket" Richard's younger brother. Only 5' 7", Henri was nearly Maurice's equal as a player. Henri, nicknamed "the Pocket Rocket," scored 1,046 points with the Montreal Canadiens during a career that lasted from 1955 to 1975.

notorious nicknames

Tough defenseman "Bad Joe" Hall hated his nickname. Center Max Bentley was called Pinocchio because of his long nose. Another defenseman, Vladimir Konstantinov, is known as the Impaler because of his stick work. These players had less than complimentary nicknames.

1. THE PUCK GOESINSKI

Steve Buzinski was a goaltender for the New York Rangers in 1942. Buzinski gave up more than six goals a game during his nine-game career. Buzinski's goaltending was so bad that he was given the nickname Puck Goesinski.

2. HORSEFACE

Hall of Fame defenseman Kenny Reardon was nicknamed Horseface. Reardon even posed for a photograph with a plug of hay in his mouth. Reardon had two other unflattering nicknames, "Big Ox" and "Butcher."

3. TERRIBLE

"Terrible" Ted Lindsay earned his nickname because of his terrible temper. Lindsay was one of hockey's best players and one of the most feared. The 5′ 8″ left winger skated quickly and carried a big stick that he called "the Great Equalizer." Lindsay was also known as "Scarface." During his 17-year career, Lindsay received more than 700 stitches in his face.

4. THE GARBAGE MAN

Steve Shutt led the NHL in goals scored with 60 during the 1976–1977 season. The Montreal left winger scored 424 goals during his Hall of Fame career. He picked up the nickname the Garbage Man because he netted so many garbage goals on rebound shots.

5. THE TOURIST

Edwin McGregor was nicknamed the Tourist because he played for so many teams. In 1911 alone, McGregor played for five different teams.

6. SUITCASE

Another much traded player was Gary Smith. The goalie played for Toronto, Oakland, Chicago, Vancouver, Minnesota, Washington, and Winnipeg between 1965 and 1980. His frequent travels earned him the nickname Suitcase. Smith's NHL record was 173 wins, 261 losses, and 74 ties.

7. KILLER

Alex Kaleta was a left winger who played with the New York Rangers from 1948 to 1951. New York fans sarcastically gave him the nickname Killer because of his reluctance to mix it up in the corners.

8. MURDER

Don Murdoch had one of the most intimidating nicknames in hockey. Murdoch played right wing for the

New York Rangers from 1976 to 1980. His nickname, Murder, was a play on his last name.

9. PUNCH

Punch Imlach had a Hall of Fame career and was coach of the Toronto Maple Leafs from 1958 to 1969. Imlach got his nickname while as a player. He was knocked out during a game and when he came to in the dressing room, Imlach took a punch at the trainer.

10. CEMENT HEAD

Jim Hargreaves played for the Vancouver Canucks from 1970 to 1973. He is remembered today for his nickname Cement Head. The hardheaded defenseman scored only one goal in his 66-game NHL career.

Dipsy Doodle Dandies

L eft winger Mark Pavelich was known as the Fishin' Magician. Cecil Dillon, a right winger with the New York Rangers in the 1930s, was nicknamed the Thornbury Teaser. These players had some of hockey's most unusual nicknames.

1. DIPSY DOODLE DANDY FROM DELISLE

Max Bentley was a Hall of Fame center who scored 245 goals during his NHL career that lasted from 1940 to 1954. He got his nickname, the Dipsy Doodle Dandy from Delisle, because he was from Delisle, Saskatchewan. The Dipsy Doodle Dandy was renowned for his fast skating and sensational stickhandling that enabled him to slip past defenders.

2. THE CHICOUTIMI CUCUMBER

Georges Vezina was born in Chicoutimi, Quebec, in 1887. The Hall of Fame goaltender was known as the Chicoutimi Cucumber because he was as cool as a cucumber on the ice. The Vezina Trophy, awarded annually to the NHL's best goaltender, was named in his honor.

3. **BLINKY**

Detroit Red Wings right winger Gordie Howe fractured his skull and lacerated his right eye when he crashed headfirst into the boards during a 1959 Stanley Cup game against Toronto. Emergency surgery saved his life, but the injury left him with a permanent tick. Howe was given the nickname Blinky because of his involuntary blinking.

4. **THE COUNT OF SAUERKRAUT**

Milt Schmidt played on the Boston Bruins' famed Kraut Line with Woody Dumart and Bobby Bauer. Schmidt, the National Hockey League's leading scorer in 1940, was nicknamed the Count of Sauerkraut.

5. **OLD BOOTNOSE**

Hall of Fame center Sid Abel played for the Detroit Red Wings and Chicago Black Hawks from 1938 to 1954. He received his nickname, Old Bootnose, after Maurice Richard punched him, breaking his nose in two places.

6. **APPLE CHEEKS**

Harry Lumley was only 17 years old when he played his first game with the Detroit Red Wings in 1943. The young goalie was nicknamed Apple Cheeks because of his rosy cheeks.

7. **GUMP**

Lorne Worsley was one of hockey's best goalies and one of the sport's most colorful characters. Worsley won 335 games during his NHL career, from 1952 to 1974. He was nicknamed Gump as a child because he resembled the comic strip character Andy Gump.

8. THE EMBALMER

Alf Pike played left wing and center for the New York Rangers from 1939 to 1947. The rugged Pike was nicknamed the Embalmer.

9. THE SLUMBERING ROMEO

Frank Finnigan of the Ottawa Senators was one of the best right wings of the 1920s. Born in Shawville, Quebec, he was nicknamed the Shawville Express. He also had a more unusual nickname, the Slumbering Romeo.

10. THE STRATFORD TEETHPULLER

Bill Carson, a center with the Stratford Indians, was the Ontario Hockey Association's leading scorer in 1925. Though many hockey players lose their teeth by fighting or being hit with a puck or stick, Carson pulled teeth during his off-season job as a dentist. Carson was nicknamed the Stratford Teethpuller.

They're Animals

G oaltender Emile Francis was nicknamed the Cat because of his catlike reflexes. One of the fastest skaters in hockey during the 1940s, Leo Gravelle was known as the Gazelle. Another speedy skater, center Charley McVeigh, was nicknamed Rabbit. John McCormack, a center who played with Toronto, Montreal, and Chicago, was nicknamed Goose because of his long neck. Marcel Dionne, who scored more than 700 goals during his NHL career, was called Little Beaver. The players in this list all have animal nicknames.

1. **THE PORT PERRY WOODPECKER**

John Ross Roach was the first goaltender in the history of the NHL to win 200 games. The Detroit Red Wings' goalie won game 200 on March 9, 1933. Born in Port Perry, Ontario, Roach's nickname was the Port Perry Woodpecker.

2. **CAMILLE THE EEL**

New York Rangers center Camille Henry finished second to Gordie Howe in goals scored during the 1962–

1963 season. Henry was nicknamed Camille the Eel because of his slippery moves.

3. TURK

Walter Broda was nicknamed Turk because his neck turned beet red when he was angry. The Hall of Famer was no turkey as a goalie, especially in the playoffs. From 1936 to 1952, the Toronto Maple Leafs' goaltender recorded an amazing 1.98 goals against average in the Stanley Cup playoffs.

Broda's neck turned red whenever he was the victim of a prank. On one occasion, his teammates played a practical joke on their gullible goalie. During a clubhouse meeting, Broda was told that they had found a week-old baby. The players were instructed to stand up if they wanted to claim the baby. What Broda did not know was that his chair had been rigged with a small electric charge. When Broda was shocked, he stood up. He was handed a baby pig wrapped in a blanket.

4. RAT

Harry Westwick was the star rover for the great Ottawa Silver Seven teams at the turn of the twentieth century. In 1905, Westwick scored 24 goals in 13 games. He was nicknamed Rat because a Quebec sportswriter described him as a "miserable, insignificant rat."

5. SHRIMP

At 5′ 3″ and 135 pounds, Roy Worters was one of the smallest players in NHL history. The goalie was nicknamed Shrimp because he was so tiny. Despite his small size, Worters was a Hall of Fame goalie with an outstanding career goals against average of 2.27.

6. BLACK CAT

Johnny Gagnon played right wing with the Montreal Canadiens in the 1930s. He was nicknamed Black Cat because he had black hair and catlike moves on the ice.

7. BIG BIRD

Montreal Canadiens Larry Robinson played in 10 NHL All Star games between 1974 and 1992. The 6'4" defenseman was nicknamed Big Bird because he resembled the Sesame Street character.

8. HOUND DOG

Left wing Bob Kelly was one of the Broad Street Bullies on the powerful Philadelphia Flyers teams of the 1970s. Kelly, who dogged opposing players with his tenacity, was nicknamed Hound Dog.

9. JAKE THE SNAKE

Jacques Plante was one of hockey's greatest goaltenders. Plante won 434 games and lost only 247 during his NHL career that spanned from 1952 to 1973. He was nicknamed Jake the Snake because he frequently snaked away from the crease to grab the puck and pass it off to a teammate.

10. MOUSE

Stan Mikita was a star right wing with the Chicago Black Hawks for more than 20 seasons. He was nicknamed Mouse because of a chant that came from the Chicago fans. They would spell out M-I-K-I-T-A M-O-U-S-E whenever he would make a good play. Mikita made a lot of good plays, as his 1,467 career points attest.

Production Lines

Many of hockey's best forward lines have had their own nicknames. The Dynamite Line was the 1920's Boston Bruins line of Cooney Weiland, Dutch Gainor, and Dit Clapper. The postwar New York Rangers line was called the Atomic Line. A Rangers line of the 1950s, headed by hard shooting Andy Bathgate, was known as the Firing Squad. The high-scoring Triple Crown Line of the Los Angeles Kings, consisting of Marcel Dionne, Dave Taylor, and Charlie Simmer, scored 161 goals during the 1980–1981 season. Some other noteworthy lines included the A Line, Razzle Dazzle Line, Diaper Line, Fossil Line, Hot Line, and the Long Island Lighting Company Line. The 1985 Edmonton Oilers line of Wally Lindstrom, Billy Carroll, and Dave Semenko was referred to as Willy, Billy, and Silly.

1. PRODUCTION LINE

Detroit is famed for its automobile production lines. Over the years the Detroit Red Wings have called their high-scoring forward lines the Production Line. The most famous Production Line included Gordie Howe, Ted Lindsay, and Sid Abel.

2. PUNCH LINE

One of the greatest forward lines in hockey history was the Punch Line of the Montreal Canadiens in the 1940s. Opponents soon learned that the Punch Line was no joke. The players packing the punch were right wing Maurice Richard, left wing Toe Blake, and center Elmer Lach.

3. BREAD LINE

Bread lines were common in the Great Depression to feed the hungry. During the 1930s the New York Rangers' forward line was also known as the Bread Line. The name derived because the scoring line of Mac Colville, Neil Colville, and Alex Shibicky was the bread and butter of the team.

4. G-A-G LINE

The New York Rangers' trio of Vic Hadfield, Jean Ratelle, and Rod Gilbert was known as the G-A-G Line. The G-A-G stood for Goal-A-Game. In 1972, Hadfield, Ratelle, and Gilbert combined for 138 goals.

5. HEM LINE

The HEM line was a Toronto Maple Leafs forward line of the 1950s and 1960s, consisting of Billy Harris, Gerry Ehman, and Frank Mahovlich. The nickname came from the first letter of each of their last names. A later Chicago Black Hawks line of Bobby Hull, Phil Esposito, and Chico Maki was also named the HEM Line.

6. MPH LINE

One of the most feared Chicago front lines was the MPH Line. The 1960s line included Stan Mikita, Jim Pappin, and Bobby Hull. The swift skating line also got their nickname from the first letters of their last names.

7. KID LINE

Joe Primeau, Charlie Conacher, and Harvey Jackson were a young forward line of the Toronto Maple Leafs, known as the Kid Line. During the 1931–1932 season, the trio finished first, second, and fourth in the NHL in scoring.

8. FRENCH CONNECTION

The French Connection was a popular movie of the early 1970s. The Buffalo Sabres named the forward line "the French Connection." The French Connection were Gil Perreault, Rene Robert, and Rick Martin.

9. MAFIA LINE

The New York Rangers' Mafia Line was made up of Phil Esposito, Don Maloney, and Don Murdoch. Esposito was the Godfather and his linesmates were the Two Dons.

10. PONY LINE

Chicago's Pony Line was one of the best forward lines of the 1940s. Members of the Pony Line were Max Bentley, Doug Bentley, and Bill Mosienko. The Pony Line, one of the fastest in NHL history, ran like wild horses over opposing defenders.

Family Affairs

In 1921, Cy Denneny of the Ottawa Senators scored six goals in a game. That same year, brother Corb, playing for the Toronto St. Patricks, also scored six goals in a game. In a February 22, 1981, game against the Washington Capitals, Peter Stastny of the Quebec Nordiques scored four goals and had four assists. In the same game, his brother and teammate Anton Stastny scored three goals and had five assists in the 11-7 Quebec victory. On March 20, 1971, brothers Ken and Dave Dryden played goalie against each other in a game between Montreal and Buffalo. The Patricks were known as the Royal Family of Hockey because so many members of the family played professional hockey.

1. **THE HOWES**

Gordie Howe played on the same team with his sons, Marty and Mark, for six seasons in the World Hockey Association (WHA). The Howes played together on the Houston Aeros and New England Whalers. During the 1979–1980 season, the Howes played on the Hartford Whalers of the National Hockey League.

2. THE HULLS

Bobby Hull scored 610 goals during his illustrious career. During the 1970–1971 season, Bobby and his brother Dennis became the first siblings to score 40 goals in the same season. Bobby's son, Brett, has also scored more than 600 goals during his NHL career. Brett concluded that his success "must be in the genes."

3. THE RICHARDS

Maurice "the Rocket" Richard of the Montreal Canadiens was one of the greatest players in hockey history. Although it was a tough act to follow, his younger brother, Henri "the Pocket Rocket" Richard, also had a Hall of Fame career in Montreal.

4. THE ESPOSITOS

Phil Esposito was one of the most prolific scorers in NHL history, while his brother Tony was one of the best players at preventing goals. Phil scored 717 goals while playing for the Chicago Black Hawks, Boston Bruins, and New York Rangers. Tony won 423 games and recorded 76 shutouts while guarding the net for the Montreal Canadiens and Chicago Black Hawks.

5. THE SMITHS

Seven members of the Smith family played professional hockey. Two of the Smith brothers, Alf and Harry, were stars on the outstanding Ottawa teams in the first decade of the twentieth century. Alf and Harry were two of hockey's roughest players. Alf was nicknamed Dirty Alf and was once tried for assault after knocking out Montreal's Hod Stuart with his stick. In

London Life-Portnoy/Hockey Hall of Fame

Phil Esposito (shown above) was adept at scoring goals, and his brother Tony specialized in stopping them as a goalkeeper.

that same 1907 game, Harry broke Ernie Johnson's nose with a high stick. Another brother, Tommy, led three different hockey leagues in scoring and once scored eight goals in a game.

6. THE SUTTERS

The Sutter family produced six brothers who played in the National Hockey League; Brent, Rich, Ron, Brian,

Duane, and Darryl were all on NHL rosters between 1982 and 1987. Both Brent and Brian scored more than 300 goals during their careers.

7. THE PLAGERS

The Plager brothers, Barclay, Bill, and Bob, all played for the St. Louis Blues. As children, the Plager brothers perfected their boxing skills by putting socks over their fists and fighting in the backyard. Older brother Barclay beat up Bill, who then would proceed across the street and punch his cousins, who had no idea why he was taking it out on them. In a junior hockey game between Peterborough and Guelph, Barclay and younger brother Bob fought on the ice and carried their battle over into the stands. During his hockey career, Barclay Plager had his nose broken 10 times. Plager's father was nicknamed Squirrel because he raised three "nuts."

8. THE HEXTALLS

Bryan Hextall was an All Star right wing who played for the New York Rangers from 1936 to 1948. He led the NHL in scoring in 1942. His sons, Bryan Jr. and Dennis, played in the NHL in the 1960s and 1970s. Bryan's grandson, Ron, was a star goalie who won the Vezina and Conn Smythe trophies with the Philadelphia Flyers in 1987.

9. THE CONACHERS

Charlie Conacher led the NHL in goals scored five times between 1931 and 1936. His brother, Roy, was the league's leading scorer in 1949. A third brother, Lionel "the Big Train" Conacher, was a Hall of Fame defenseman who played in the NHL from 1925 to 1937.

10. THE BENTLEYS

Brothers Doug and Max Bentley starred for the Chicago
Black Hawks during the 1940s. On January 28, 1943,
Max scored four goals in one period in a game against
the New York Rangers. Doug assisted on all four goals.
Both Max and Doug were elected to the Hockey Hall of
Fame.

The International Hockey League

Throughout its history, the National Hockey League has been dominated by Canadian-born players. In recent years, stars from Europe have joined NHL rosters. Dominik Hasek, Peter Stastny, Borje Salming, Teemu Selanne, Pavel Bure, and Sergei Federov are some of the outstanding European players who have starred in the NHL.

1. SWEENEY SCHRINER

Sweeney Schriner was born in Russia in 1911. Raised in Calgary, Schriner led the NHL in scoring in 1936 and 1937 while playing left wing for the New York Americans.

2. TOM ANDERSON

Born in Edinburgh, Scotland, in 1910, Tom Anderson played left wing and defenseman for Detroit, New York, and Brooklyn from 1934 to 1942. In 1942, while playing for the Brooklyn Americans, Anderson won the Hart Trophy as the NHL's Most Valuable Player. When the Brooklyn franchise folded at the end of the 1942 season, Anderson retired from the NHL at the peak of his career.

3. SVEN JOHANSON

One of the first European players signed by an NHL team was Swedish star Sven Johanson. The Boston Bruins had high hopes for him when he was brought to America more than 30 years ago. In the locker room, Johanson decided to play a prank on his new team-mates. He switched the players' false teeth. Apparently the Bruins were not amused—Johanson was sent back to Sweden a few days later.

4. JOE HALL

Joe Hall was a Hall of Fame defenseman who was born in Staffordshire, England, in 1882. The Montreal Cana-dien star fell ill with the Spanish influenza during the 1919 Stanley Cup finals and died on April 5, 1919.

5. TOM DUNDERDALE

Tom Dunderdale is the only player born in Australia to be elected to the Hockey Hall of Fame. The center/rover starred in the Pacific Coast Hockey Association (PCHA) in the 1910s.

6. ROD LANGWAY

Defenseman Rod Langway was born in Formosa, a country known today as Taiwan. Langway won the James Norris Memorial Trophy as the NHL's best de-fenseman while playing for the Washington Capitals in 1983 and 1984.

7. JARI KURRI

One of the best hockey players ever to come from Eu-rope, Jari Kurri was born in Helsinki, Finland. The right winger won five Stanley Cups with the Edmonton Oilers and led the NHL in goals scored with 68 in 1986. The eight-time All Star finished his career with 601 goals.

8. JAROMIR JAGR

Jaromir Jagr is one of the best players ever to come from Czechoslovakia. In 1995, the Pittsburgh Penguins' right wing became the first European-trained player to lead the NHL in scoring. Jagr scored 62 goals and scored 149 points during the 1995–1996 season.

9. UWE KRUPP

Uwe Krupp was drafted by the Buffalo Sabres in 1983. The 6'6" defenseman from Cologne, Germany, was an All Star in 1991.

10. TOMMY WILLIAMS

American players are common in the NHL today, but for a time in the early 1960s, Tommy Williams was the only U.S.-born player in the league. The Minnesota native scored 161 goals during his career with the Boston Bruins, Minnesota North Stars, California Golden Seals, and Washington Capitals.

Born in the U.S.A.

In the past 20 years, American players have come into their own in the NHL. American-born players have won the Conn Smythe, Norris, Vezina, and Lady Byng trophies.

1. FRANK BRIMSEK

Goalie Frank Brimsek was the first American-born player to be elected to the Hockey Hall of Fame. He was awarded the Vezina Trophy and was the NHL's best goaltender in 1939 and 1942. When he retired in 1950, his career record was 252 wins, 182 losses, and 80 ties.

2. JOE MULLEN

On February 7, 1995, Joe Mullen became the first American-born player to reach 1,000 points in the NHL. Mullen reached another milestone on March 14, 1997, when he became the first American to score 500 goals. He won the Lady Byng Trophy in 1987 and 1989.

3. PAT LaFONTAINE

Despite missing most of the 1993–1994 season with a serious knee injury, Pat LaFontaine managed to score

1,013 points during his career. In 1994, the Buffalo Sabres' center scored 53 goals and 148 points.

4. CHRIS CHELIOS

Perennial All Star Chris Chelios is rated one of the best defensemen in NHL history. The defenseman from Chicago played for the Black Hawks throughout the 1990s. Chelios won the Norris Trophy as the league's best defenseman in 1989, 1993, and 1996.

5. NEAL BROTEN

Neal Broten attended the University of Minnesota and was a member of the gold-medal–winning 1980 U.S. Olympic hockey team. In 1986, Broten became the first American to score 100 points in a season. The Minnesota North Stars' center had 76 assists and 105 points.

6. BRIAN LEETCH

Born in Corpus Christi, Texas, Brian Leetch was the first American to win the Conn Smythe Trophy. The New York Rangers' defenseman was voted the Stanley Cup playoffs' Most Valuable Player in 1994. Leetch won the Norris Trophy in 1992, a year in which he passed out 80 assists and scored 102 points. Leetch won a second Norris Trophy in 1997.

7. BOB CARPENTER

Bob Carpenter was the third player selected in the 1981 NHL entry draft. In 1985, the Washington Capitals' center scored 53 goals to become the first American to score 50 goals in a season. During his long career, Carpenter scored more than 300 goals.

8. TOM BARRASSO

Tom Barrasso was only 19 years old in 1984 when the Buffalo Sabres' rookie won the Vezina Trophy as the NHL's outstanding goalie. In 1993, Barrasso led the league with 43 victories as the net tender for the Pittsburgh Penguins. On October 19, 1997, he became the first American goaltender to win 300 games.

9. TAFFY ABEL

Clarence "Taffy" Abel was the first American player to become a star in the NHL. The big defenseman from Michigan starred for the New York Rangers and Chicago Black Hawks between 1926 and 1934.

10. PHIL HOUSLEY

Phil Housley was the first American defenseman to score more than 1,000 points in his NHL career. Housley played in six NHL All Star games between 1984 and 1993.

Women in Hockey

Women's hockey debuted as an Olympic sport in 1998. The United States defeated Canada to win the event's first gold medal. Women had been playing hockey long before it became an Olympic event. Each of these women left their mark on the sport.

1. MANON RHEAUME

Manon Rheaume made hockey history when she became the only woman to play in an NHL game. Rheaume played one period as the goaltender of the Tampa Bay Lightning in an exhibition game against the St. Louis Blues on September 23, 1992. She gave up two goals and made nine saves in a 6-4 defeat. Rheaume reportedly turned down $75,000 to pose nude in *Playboy*. She was the goaltender on the Canadian Olympic team that won a silver medal at the 1998 Nagano Winter Olympics.

2. ERIN WHITTEN

Erin Whitten was the first woman goalie to win a pro hockey game. On October 30, 1993, Whitten was in goal for the Toledo Storm in a 6-5 victory over the Dayton Bombers in an East Coast Hockey League (ECHL) game.

3. KATE SMITH

Singer Kate Smith was an unlikely good-luck charm for the 1974 Philadelphia Flyers. The team discovered that, for some reason, they played better when a recording of Smith singing "God Bless America" was played. Smith even performed the song in person on a few occasions. The team's record with Smith singing was 37-3-1.

4. AUBERTINE LAPANSEE

Aubertine Lapansee was the best woman hockey player in Canada during the 1910s. While playing for the Cornwall Vics from 1915 to 1917, she scored more than 80 percent of her team's goals. Although she was a great skater and scorer, she retired from the sport in 1917, since there was no way at the time she could support herself playing hockey. Many years later, she underwent a sex-change operation.

5. ABIGAIL HOFFMAN

In 1955, an 8-year-old named Ab Hoffman was selected for the All Star team of a Canadian boy's league. It was discovered that Ab Hoffman was actually a girl named Abigail. An extraordinary athlete, Hoffman finished eighth in the women's 800-meter run at the 1972 Munich Summer Olympic games.

6. LADY BYNG

Lady Byng was the wife of Canada's governor-general, Baron Byng. A hockey fan, she was especially appreciative of sportsmanlike behavior. Since 1925, the Lady Byng Trophy has been awarded annually to the player in the NHL who exhibited the best sportsmanship.

7. MARGUERITE NORRIS

The only woman to have her name inscribed on the Stanley Cup was Marguerite Norris. She had her name inscribed on the trophy after the team she owned, the Detroit Red Wings, won the Stanley Cup. The Norris family purchased the Red Wings in 1932 and the team won their first Stanley Cup in 1936.

8. LILY MURPHY

The first woman to inscribe her name on the Stanley Cup was Lily Murphy. A member of an Ottawa social club, she had somehow scratched her name on the Cup.

9. JOAN PALMER

During the 1990s, the Winnipeg Jets held a contest during intermission. A fan was selected to attempt to shoot a 3-inch puck through a $3^3/_4$-inch opening from 120 feet. A 48-year-old grandmother named Joan Palmer won $58,000 by making the nearly impossible shot.

10. JANET JONES

Hockey's superstar Wayne Gretzky married actress Janet Jones. When Gretzky was traded from the Edmonton Oilers to the Los Angeles Kings, many fans believed Gretzky had asked to be traded to Los Angeles so his wife could live closer to Hollywood, the center of the movie industry. During the 2002 Winter Olympics, Jones stood beside Gretzky cheering for Canada versus the United States, showing that rather than "Americanizing" Gretzky, he had instead in a way "Canadianized" her.

Black Hockey Stars

I n the 1920s, NHL president Frank Calder insisted that there be no color barrier in the National Hockey League. Color barrier or not, it would be 1958 before the first black player appeared in an NHL game. The Calgary Flames' right wing Jarome Iginla was the NHL's top scorer during the 2001–2002 NHL season.

1. WILLIE O'REE

On January 18, 1958, Willie O'Ree of the Boston Bruins became the first black athlete to play in an NHL game. In that game, Boston defeated the Montreal Canadiens 3-0. O'Ree played in only two games that year before returning to minor league hockey. O'Ree returned to the Bruins for the 1960–1961 season and scored four goals and 10 assists in 43 games. O'Ree was sent back to the minors and, although he never played again in the NHL, he continued playing in other professional leagues until 1979. Following O'Ree's breaking of the hockey color barrier, it would be another 13 years before another black player saw action in the NHL.

2. HERB CARNEGIE

Herb Carnegie was probably the best black hockey player *never* to play in the NHL. Carnegie was a three-time Most Valuable Player in the Quebec Senior League. Conn Smythe of the Toronto Maple Leafs said of Carnegie, "I'd sign him in a minute, if I could only turn him white." In 1947, the same year Jackie Robinson broke major league baseball's color barrier, Carnegie was offered a minor league contract by the New York Rangers. Carnegie turned it down because he could make more money playing for Quebec.

3. GRANT FUHR

Grant Fuhr was the NHL's first black superstar. The goaltender for the great Edmonton Oilers teams of the 1980s, he played on four Stanley Cup winners. Fuhr set an NHL record for goalies by playing in 79 games during the 1995–1996 season with the St. Louis Blues. Fuhr won more than 400 games in the net during his career.

4. TONY McKEGNEY

Left wing Tony McKegney was the first black player to be a prolific scorer in the NHL. He scored 40 goals during the 1987–1988 season with the St. Louis Blues. McKegney finished his NHL career in 1991 with 320 career goals.

5. MIKE MARSON

Mike Marson was a left wing signed by the Washington Capitals in 1974. He scored 24 goals during his six NHL seasons. Marson did not wear underpants on the ice and when he sweated, the white pants became almost transparent. As a result, the Capitals changed their pants color to blue.

6. BILL RILEY

Right wing Bill Riley was a teammate of Mike Marson on the Washington Capitals from 1975 to 1979. He scored 31 goals during his five-year NHL career. Riley endured racial taunts early in his career and fought more than 100 times in the minor leagues.

7. BUD KELLY

Bud Kelly was one of the first outstanding black hockey players. A star of the 1910s, he was seriously scouted by the NHL's Toronto St. Patricks. Unfortunately, they never signed him.

8. HIPPO GALLOWAY

Hippo Galloway played for Woodstock of the Central Ontario Hockey League (COHL) at the end of the nineteenth century. He was the first black to play in the league. In one game against Hamilton, Galloway scored two goals.

9. CHARLEY LIGHTFOOT

Charley Lightfoot was the second black player in the Central Ontario Hockey Association (COHA). Lightfoot played for Stratford. He gave up his promising hockey career to join a barnstorming baseball team.

10. DONALD BRASHEAR

Left wing Donald Brashear was one of the toughest players in the NHL during the 1990s. During the 1997–1998 season, while playing for the Vancouver Canucks, Brashear led the league with 372 penalty minutes. In February 2000, Brashear was injured when Marty Mc-Sorley of the Boston Bruins hit him on the head with his stick.

The Smart Set

H all of Fame left wing Frank Mahovlich said, "I have the body of an athlete and the mind of a librarian." Clint Albright, a center who played with the New York Rangers in the late 1940s, was nicknamed the Professor because of his interest in intellectual pursuits. Art Ross, who had a distinguished career in hockey as a player, coach, and executive, was called "the Brain" because of his innovative ideas. The players and coaches in this section demonstrated brains as well as brawn.

1. GEORGE PLIMPTON

George Plimpton is the publisher of the literary magazine the *Paris Review*. Plimpton was the author of a best-seller, *Paper Lion,* about his tryouts with the football team the Detroit Lions. In 1977, Plimpton decided to try his hand at professional hockey. The Boston Bruins permitted Plimpton to play goalie for five minutes in an exhibition game against the Philadelphia Flyers, one of the best teams in the league. Plimpton gave up a goal on the first shot taken, but he held the Flyers scoreless for the remainder of the five minutes. Plimpton made several saves, survived a power play, and even stopped Reg Leach, one of the NHL's leading scorers, on a penalty shot.

2. KEN DRYDEN

Ken Dryden was not only one of the greatest goaltenders in NHL history, he was one of the game's smartest players. Dryden played college hockey at Cornell, an Ivy League school, and earned his law degree at McGill University. Dryden was the author of *The Game*, one of the best books about hockey. Dryden amazed his teammates with his knowledge. Rick Wamsley said that by the time Dryden finished answering questions, he had forgotten what question had been asked.

3. SYL APPS

Syl Apps was a star center with the Toronto Maple Leafs from 1936 to 1948. Apps was his high school's valedictorian and he attended McMaster University. Following his hockey career, Apps became a successful politician in Canada.

4. RED BERENSON

Red Berenson scored 261 goals during his NHL career that lasted from 1962 to 1978. A college graduate, Berenson was known for his love of reading. New York Rangers coach Emile Francis did not appreciate his pursuit of knowledge. Francis once threatened to throw Berenson off the team bus if he ever caught him reading a book again.

5. JOHN GARRETT

John Garrett was a goaltender in the NHL from 1979 to 1985. He was known for his eccentric study of languages. He studied Latin via a correspondence course. When asked why he was interested in a language no longer spoken, he replied, "If I meet an ancient Roman, just think of the great conversation I can have with him." Garrett also studied Hebrew.

6. HOBART BAKER

Hobart Baker was considered the first great American hockey player. Baker starred for Princeton from 1910 to 1914 and led his university to two collegiate hockey titles. A scholar as well as an athlete, Baker was admired by Princeton classmate F. Scott Fitzgerald. Fitzgerald, the author of *The Great Gatsby*, wrote of Baker, "An ideal worthy of everything in my enthusiastic admiration, yet consummated and expressed in a human being who stood within ten feet of me." Baker was a charter member of the Hockey Hall of Fame in 1945.

7. MIKE KEENAN

Mike Keenan earned a master's degree in education from the University of Toronto. Known for his analytical approach to coaching, Keenan led the New York Rangers to the Stanley Cup title in 1994, their first in 54 years.

8. BILL MASTERTON

Bill Masterton received a master's degree in finance from the University of Denver. Masterton played center for the Minnesota North Stars during the 1967–1968 season. Following his hockey career, Masterton hoped to pursue a career in business. Tragically, he died at the age of 29 on January 15, 1968, as the result of a head injury suffered during a game.

9. **GORDON ROBERTS**

During the 1916–1917 season, left wing Gordon Roberts scored 43 goals in 23 games to set a PCHA scoring record. He scored 203 goals during his 166-game professional career. The gentlemanly Roberts would help up and apologize to any opposing player knocked to the ice. In 1916, Roberts received his medical degree from McGill University. For several seasons he continued to play hockey while practicing medicine in the off-season. Roberts was elected to the Hockey Hall of Fame in 1971.

10. **RUSSELL BOWIE**

Russell Bowie was the most prolific scorer of the first decade of the twentieth century. During that time he averaged an unbelievable three goals a game. Bowie remained an amateur throughout his career, turning down large sums of money to turn professional. He had a great appreciation of music, and the Montreal Wanderers unsuccessfully tried to entice him by offering him a grand piano if he signed with them. Bowie was elected to the Hockey Hall of Fame in 1945.

Playing Politics

H ockey stars are national heroes in Canada. Several players have gone on to successful political careers after hanging up their skates.

1. WENDELL ANDERSON

In the first WHA draft in 1972, the Minnesota Fighting Saints selected Wendell Anderson. What made the choice unusual was that Anderson was the governor of Minnesota at the time. The 36-year-old politician had been a member of the U.S. hockey team that had won a silver medal at the 1956 Winter Olympic Games. Anderson declined the offer to play in the NHL and served out his term as governor.

2. SYL APPS

After playing with the Toronto Maple Leafs for 10 seasons, Syl Apps had a long career in politics. Apps served as corrections minister in the Canadian cabinet. From 1963 to 1980, he was a member of the Ontario parliament, representing Kingston and the Islands.

3. RED KELLY

Red Kelly played on eight Stanley Cup championship teams and won his share of political campaigns. Kelly won a seat in the Canadian House of Commons representing the York West district. From 1962 to 1965, Kelly played professional hockey for the Toronto Maple Leafs in addition to his job as a legislator.

4. LIONEL CONACHER

Defenseman Lionel Conacher played a dozen seasons in the NHL. He retired from hockey in 1937 and was elected to the Ontario legislature that same year. Conacher was elected to the Canadian House of Commons in 1949 and occupied the seat until his death in 1954.

5. HOWIE MEEKER

In 1947, Howie Meeker won the Calder Memorial Trophy as the outstanding rookie in the NHL. On January 18, 1947, the Toronto Maple Leafs right wing scored five goals in a game. The popular player served as a member of the parliament in Ottawa from 1951 to 1953.

6. BUCKO McDONALD

Wilfred "Bucko" McDonald was a hard-hitting defenseman who played in the NHL from 1934 to 1945. Following his hockey career, he became a politician with the Liberal Party. McDonald was elected to the legislature representing the Parry Sound–Musoka district.

7. FRANK MAHOVLICH

Frank Mahovlich scored 533 goals during his Hall of Fame career. In 1998, Mahovlich was appointed to the Canadian Senate by Prime Minister Jean Chretien.

8. GEORGE HAINSWORTH

One of the NHL's stingiest goaltenders, George Hainsworth set a record when he recorded 22 shutouts during the 1928–1929 season. After his retirement from hockey, Hainsworth was elected alderman in Kitchener, Ontario.

9. ALAN EAGLESON

From 1963 to 1967, Alan Eagleson served as a member of the Provincial Parliament in the Ontario government. For eight years he was the president of the Conservative Party. Eagleson was the founder of the NHL Players Association and the man most responsible for promoting the Summit Series between Canada and the Soviet Union. His reputation was later tarnished with revelations that he had embezzled from the players' pension fund. In 1998, he became the first person to have his plaque removed from the Hockey Hall of Fame.

10. DENNIS MURPHY

Dennis Murphy was a Canadian politician at the turn of the twentieth century. Although he had no connection with hockey, he somehow got his name inscribed on the Stanley Cup.

Sports of All Sorts

Hockey Hall of Fame player Aurel Joliat was a star fullback for the Ottawa Rough Riders. Cecil Dye, the NHL's leading scorer during the 1922–1923 season, played minor league baseball and was nicknamed Babe because of his baseball skills. Hockey great Syl Apps finished sixth in the men's pole vault at the 1936 Berlin Summer Olympics. Center Todd Bergen left the Philadelphia Flyers in 1985 to pursue a career on the Professional Golfers Association (PGA) Tour. Hall of Fame goalie Bill Durnan was a premier fast-pitch softball pitcher who once struck out 24 batters in a game. Nick Fotiu, a left wing who played 13 seasons in the NHL, was a Golden Gloves boxing champion in Rhode Island. Here are 10 more multisport stars.

1. LIONEL CONACHER

Lionel Conacher was voted Canada's male athlete of the first half of the twentieth century. The Big Train was also voted Canada's greatest football player of the half century. Conacher was elected to the Canadian Sports Hall of Fame in 1955, the Canadian Football Hall of

Fame in 1963, the Canadian Lacrosse Hall of Fame in 1966, and the Hockey Hall of Fame in 1994.

2. DAN BAIN

Dan Bain led Winnipeg to the Stanley Cup titles in 1896 and 1901. During the 1901 Stanley Cup playoffs he was nicknamed the Masked Man because he wore a wooden mask to protect his broken nose. The center was a charter member of the Hockey Hall of Fame in 1945. An exceptional athlete, Bain excelled in several sports. He was Canada's top trap shooter, Manitoba's cycling and roller skating champion, and Winnipeg's best gymnast. The versatile Bain was also a pairs figure skating champion and one of the best lacrosse players of his time.

3. JAROSLAV DROBNY

Jaroslav Drobny was a member of the Czechoslova-kian world-champion hockey team in 1947. A world-class tennis player, Drobny won the French Open men's singles titles in 1951 and 1952 and was the Wimbledon men's champion in 1954.

4. BILL EZINICKI

"Wild Bill" Ezinicki played right wing for the Toronto Maple Leafs, Boston Bruins, and New York Rangers. He retired from the NHL in 1955 to become a professional golfer. His best tournament on the PGA was a second-place finish in the Bob Hope Classic.

5. HARVEY PULFORD

One of Canada's most talented all-around athletes, Harvey Pulford was captain of the legendary Ottawa Silver Seven teams that won three Stanley Cups in the first decade of the twentieth century. The defenseman was elected to the Hockey Hall of Fame in 1945. Pulford was also captain of the Ottawa Rough Riders' championship football teams of 1898, 1899, and 1900. He was also a heavyweight boxing champion in eastern Canada, a member of the champion Ottawa Capitals' lacrosse team, and a world-class rower.

6. JOHN HUTTON

John Bouse Hutton was the goaltender for the Ottawa Silver Seven Stanley Cup championship team in 1903 and 1904. He played fullback for the Ottawa Rough Riders' football team and was goaltender for the Ottawa Capitals' lacrosse team. In 1904, he became the only athlete to play on Canadian championship teams in hockey, football, and lacrosse in the same year.

7. EDDIE JOHNSTON

Eddie Johnston was a goaltender for the Boston Bruins from 1962 to 1973. In the early 1970s he reached a contract impasse. Johnston felt he deserved a raise to $20,000. Bruins vice president Charles Mulcahy agreed to a golf challenge to decide the issue. If Johnston won, Mulcahy would double his salary to $40,000. If he lost, he would not receive a raise. Mulcahy had won several golf tournaments and had represented the United States in international competitions, so he believed he was a cinch to win the three-hole competition. What he did not realize was that Johnston was also a scratch golfer. Johnston won the bet and more than doubled his salary.

8. BILL STEWART

Bill Stewart was a major league baseball umpire for 22 seasons. Stewart was an NHL referee for nine years. In his first season as coach of the Chicago Black Hawks, Stewart led his team to the 1938 Stanley Cup title. The next season he was fired and he never coached in the NHL again.

9. NEWSY LALONDE

Newsy Lalonde led the NHL in scoring in 1919 and 1921. The Montreal Canadiens' center was elected to the Hockey Hall of Fame in 1950. That same year he was named Canada's greatest lacrosse player of the first half of the twentieth century.

10. DOUG HARVEY

Doug Harvey was not only one of the greatest defensemen in NHL history, he was talented in other sports. Harvey was offered professional contracts in baseball and football. He was also the heavyweight boxing champion of the Canadian navy.

Going for the Gold

I ce hockey became an Olympic sport in 1920 at the Antwerp Summer Olympics. When the first Winter Olympics were held at Chamonix in 1924, ice hockey became one of the premier sports at the Winter Games. The following Olympic moments are worthy of gold medals.

1. 1980 UNITED STATES HOCKEY TEAM

Prior to the 1980 Lake Placid Winter Olympics, few believed the U.S. hockey team had a chance to medal. The powerful team from the Soviet Union had won four consecutive gold medals and was the overwhelming favorite to add a fifth. In a pre-Olympic exhibition game, the Soviets crushed the Americans 10-3. The rematch occurred in the Olympic semifinal game. With ten minutes remaining in the third period, Mike Eruzione fired a 30-foot shot past Soviet goaltender Vladimir Myshkin to give the United States an upset 4-3 victory. Two days later, the United States defeated Finland 4-2 to win the gold medal. Announcer Al Michaels asked millions of jubilant American television viewers, "Do you believe in miracles?"

2.   1924 CANADIAN HOCKEY TEAM

The Toronto Granites, the best amateur hockey team in Canada, represented the country at the 1924 Chamonix Winter Olympic games. The Canadians dominated the competition. They defeated Czechoslovakia 30-0, Sweden 22-0, Switzerland 33-0, Great Britain 19-2, and the United States 6-1 to win the gold medal. Harry Watson scored 38 goals in five games, an average of more than 7 goals a game. Goaltender Jack Cameron was so bored by the one-sided matches that he once left the goal untended and skated to the boards to talk to two attractive female fans.

3.   1948 UNITED STATES HOCKEY TEAM

The United States sent two hockey teams to the 1948 St. Moritz Winter Olympics. The reason for the two teams was a dispute over which organization was the governing body of amateur hockey in the United States. One team was backed by the Amateur Athletic Association (AAA), while the other was supported by the American Hockey Association (AHA). The American Hockey Association team was recognized by the Olympic officials. The Americans outscored their opponents 86 goals to 33, but failed to medal. Some of the players from the other American team sat in the stands and booed their compatriots.

4.   1920 CZECHOSLOVAKIAN HOCKEY TEAM

The 1920 Czechoslovakian hockey team won a bronze medal despite being outscored 31 to 1 in the tournament. The Czechs lost to Canada 15-0 and were routed by the United States 16-0. Czechoslovakia defeated Sweden 1-0 to win the bronze medal.

5. 1948 ITALIAN HOCKEY TEAM

The Italian team at the 1948 Chamonix Winter Games may have been the worst hockey team in Olympic history. The Italians lost all eight of their games and were outscored 156 to 24. They were routed by the United States 31-1, Sweden 23-0, Canada 21-1, Czechoslovakia 22-3, and Switzerland 16-0.

6. 1928 CANADIAN HOCKEY TEAM

The Canadian hockey team at the 1928 St. Moritz Winter Olympics was considered so unbeatable that they were the only team given a bye until the medal round. The team was composed of players from the University of Toronto. Canada defeated Sweden 11-0, Great Britain 14-0, and Switzerland 13-0 to win the gold medal.

7. 1924 UNITED STATES HOCKEY TEAM

The 1924 U.S. hockey team did not win the gold medal, despite outscoring the opposition 73 goals to 6. The United States defeated Belgium 19-0, France 22-0, Great Britain 11-0, and Sweden 20-0 before losing in the gold-medal game to Canada, 6 to 1.

8. 1936 GREAT BRITAIN HOCKEY TEAM

Great Britain upset Canada 2-1 and won the gold medal in hockey at the 1936 Garmisch-Partenkirchen Winter Olympics. It was Canada's only defeat in hockey between 1920 and 1952. During that period, the Canadians won 37 games, lost 1, and tied 3.

9. 1948 SWISS HOCKEY FANS

The Swiss hockey fans at the 1948 St. Moritz Winter Games pelted officials with snowballs during a game between Switzerland and Canada. The rowdy fans were displeased with calls made against the Swiss team. Canada won the game 3-0 and went on to win the gold medal. Despite the vocal support of their fans, the Swiss team could do no better than a bronze medal.

10.   THE 1960 UNITED STATES HOCKEY TEAM

The gold medal won by the U.S. hockey team at the 1960 Squaw Valley Winter Olympics was just as big as a surprise as the 1980 American gold-medal–winning team. In the training tour before the Squaw Valley Olympics, the Americans lost to the University of Denver, Michigan Tech, and a team from Warroad, Minnesota. The Americans went undefeated in the Olympics, including victories over powerhouse teams from Canada and the Soviet Union.

Drinking It All In

C enter Bobby Sheehan remarked, "It wasn't that I
drank so much, it's just that I put it into such a
small body." Find out what hockey players drink.

1. GENE LEONE

In December 1951, Gene Leone, owner of the popular
Manhattan restaurant Mama Leone, proposed an unusual solution to turn around the fortunes of the slump-
ing New York Rangers. He concocted a magic elixir that
he said would turn the hapless Rangers into winners.
The mysterious solution was contained in a large black
bottle. Players took a sip from the bottle before each
game. Magically, the team began to win. They went on
an 11-game streak in which they lost only 2 games.
Word of the magic elixir spread throughout the league.
The Toronto Maple Leafs attempted to have the bottle
seized by customs at the airport. Eventually, the elixir
wore off and the Rangers returned to their losing ways.

2. HOWIE YOUNG

Defenseman Howie Young played in the NHL from
1960 to 1971. Known as "Wild Thing," Young was

known to have a taste for alcohol and a reputation for doing outrageous things. One morning, after a night out on the town, Young met a milkman making his morning rounds. Somehow he convinced the man to let him deliver the milk. Unfortunately, Young lost the delivery list. His solution was to leave a quart of milk on the doorstep of every house.

3. FRANK McCOOL

Goaltender Frank McCool had a short but memorable NHL career. In 1945, the goalie for the Toronto Maple Leafs won the Calder Trophy as the league's outstanding rookie. McCool was nicknamed Ulcers because his ulcers were so bad that he was in constant pain during the games. Between periods, McCool gulped milk to soothe his aching stomach. Despite the intense pain, McCool recorded three shutouts to lead Toronto to victory against the Detroit Red Wings in the 1945 Stanley Cup finals. The pain became too much for McCool and he retired after playing 22 games the following season.

4. NEWSY LALONDE

Hall of Fame center Newsy Lalonde nearly had his career ended before it ever started. In 1906, the promising 18-year-old was playing in the International Pro League. After injuring his leg, Lalonde took a swig from a bottle he thought contained whiskey. In fact, it was a bottle of ammonia. The liquid burned his mouth and throat and, for a time, there was concern that he might die. Miraculously, Lalonde recovered and scored two goals later in the game.

5. GUMP WORSLEY

Colorful goalie Gump Worsley was unashamedly a drinking man. When his coach commented on his beer belly, Worsley replied, "He should know better than that. He knows I only drink scotch." A reporter asked him whether it was true that he did all of his off-season training in St. Paul bars. Gump said that it was not true, "I've switched to Minneapolis bars." Despite his fondness for alcohol, Worsley won 335 games and was elected to the Hockey Hall of Fame.

6. **HERB BROOKS**

After he coached the U.S. hockey team to a surprise gold medal at the 1980 Lake Placid Winter Olympics, coach Herb Brooks was the toast of the town. One of the perks he received was an extended bar tab. Brooks recalled, "My bartender in St. Paul said I could have one free beer every day for the rest of my life. I asked him if I could bunch them up every so often, but he said, 'No!'"

7. **ERIC LINDROS**

Eric Lindros is one of the most gifted players in hockey history, but his career has been plagued by controversy. On November 29, 1992, the Philadelphia Flyers' rookie center went to a bar named Koo Koo Bananas in Whitby, Ontario. According to accounts, Lindros had a few drinks and acted a little cuckoo. A young woman claimed he poured beer on her and spat beer in her face. Lindros faced assault charges because of the incident, but he was eventually cleared of the charges.

8. **DOUG HARVEY**

Doug Harvey was one of the greatest defensemen in NHL history. He won the Norris Trophy seven times in an eight-year period between 1954 and 1962. Harvey was angered when he was not selected to the Hockey Hall of Fame the first time he was eligible. He insisted the snub was because of his drinking problem. When Harvey was elected in 1973, he boycotted the cere-monies.

9. **HOWIE MORENZ**

Howie Morenz was considered the greatest player of his day. In 1937, the Montreal center suffered a serious leg fracture in a game. The injury was considered career threatening. In the hospital, many of Morenz's friends brought him alcohol to bolster his spirits. Morenz had bottles of whiskey lined up on the counter and cases of beer stacked up under his bed. Morenz went on a drink-ing binge. On March 8, 1937, the 33-year-old player died of an embolism.

10. **HAP DAY**

Coach Clarence "Hap" Day was overjoyed when his Toronto Maple Leafs miraculously rallied from a 3-0 deficit to defeat the Detroit Red Wings in the 1942 Stan-ley Cup finals. During the celebration, Day, normally a teetotaler, indulged himself in dipping his fingers in the champagne and licking them.

Food for Thought

In the 1960s, the Detroit Red Wings kept a huge container of yogurt in the dressing room and encouraged their players to eat a scoop before each game for added energy. Jack "the Round Squire" Crawford, an All Star defenseman for the Bruins in the 1940s, started a grocery business in Boston. During the Great Depression, Detroit Red Wings general manager Jack Adams let a fan attend a game at Olympic Stadium in exchange for a five-pound bag of potatoes. Goalie "Sugar Jim" Henry got his nickname for his love of sweets. Find out what's on the menu.

1. TURK BRODA

Before the 1949 season, Toronto Maple Leafs owner Conn Smythe expressed concern with the bulging waistlines of some of his players. Star goalie Turk Broda was singled out for the most criticism. Smythe gave him an ultimatum: either lose seven pounds in a week or face serious consequences. The crash diet was referred to in the press as "The Battle of the Bulge." Fans sent him suggestions on how he could lose the weight. Broda went on a diet of grapefruit and soft-boiled eggs. He managed to lose the weight just in time and celebrated by eating a steak.

2. GEORGE MORRISON

Left wing George Morrison played for the St. Louis Blues from 1970 to 1972. One night he did not expect to play in a game against Los Angeles. During the game, he offered a vendor one of his sticks in exchange for a hot dog. Just as he took the first bite, coach Scotty Bowman sent him into the game. Morrison hid the hot dog in his glove. Near the crease, Morrison received a hard check and the hot dog flew into the air. The St. Louis goalie, thinking it was the puck, tried to catch it. There was a trail of wiener, bun, mustard, and relish on the ice. Bowman, not amused by his player's behavior, benched Morrison.

3. GAVIN KIRK

On February 25, 1973, the Ottawa Nationals played the Alberta Oilers. The Ottawa trainer found a half-eaten corn cob in the locker room and gave it to a player named Gavin Kirk. Kirk kept the cob in his glove and Ottawa won the game 2 to 1. The team considered the rotting piece of food good luck and rubbed it before each game. Ottawa won 12 of its last 13 games to secure a playoff spot.

4. HARRY MUMMERY

Harry Mummery was a hefty defenseman who played in the NHL from 1917 to 1923. Mummery moonlighted as a fireman and sometimes arrived just before a game. He would put a huge steak on a shovel and cook it in a pot-bellied stove in the dressing room. Before a game it was not uncommon for him to eat two 5-pound steaks and an apple pie. He would wash down the meal by drinking a pint of cream.

5. CY DENNENY

Cy Denneny was a high-scoring left wing for the Ottawa Senators from 1917 to 1928. On January 19, 1924, the Ottawa train, on its way to Montreal, was caught in a blizzard and became snowbound. Denneny volunteered to go look for food. He fell down a well that was covered with snow. Luckily, he escaped serious injury.

6. TIM HORTON

Toronto Maple Leafs All Star defenseman Tim Horton had a lifelong love of donuts. Horton opened a chain of donut and coffee shops that eventually grew to more than 1,700 locations.

7. GEORGE HAYES

Linesman George Hayes officiated 1,544 NHL games during his career. The 220-pounder liked to eat canned meat sandwiches on the train between cities. One night, after he drank a little too much, Hayes made and ate a sandwich from a can of dog food.

8. MIKE ILITCH

Mike Ilitch was the founder of the Little Caesars pizza chain. In 1982, Ilitch bought the Detroit Red Wings. The next year, he signed star defenseman Brad Park. As part of the deal, Ilitch awarded Park two pizza outlets.

9. EDDIE GERARD

During a game in the early 1920s between the Ottawa Senators and the Montreal Canadiens, an Ottawa fan threw an apple at Montreal's Sprague Cleghorn. The apple missed him and hit Ottawa's defenseman Eddie Gerard in the head.

10. **BUTCH BOUCHARD**

Butch Bouchard was a popular defenseman who played for the Montreal Canadiens from 1941 to 1956. When he retired, he opened a restaurant in Montreal named Chez Butch and bought a beef farm.

Bigger Is Better

Hockey players are not known for their size, but there have been exceptions. Meet some of hockey's biggest players.

1. BILLY NICHOLSON

Billy Nicholson was a goalie whose career spanned from 1901 to 1917. Although he was only 5'7", his weight ballooned to as much as 300 pounds. Nicholson was one of the first goalies to drop to the ice to make a save. Some reporters joked that the ice cracked when Nicholson plopped.

2. HARRY MUMMERY

Defenseman Harry Mummery played for Toronto, Quebec, Montreal, and Hamilton during his six-year NHL career. Mummery, known for his prodigious appetite, weighed as much as 260 pounds during his playing days.

3. TODD MacCULLOUGH

Todd MacCullough was a talented defenseman in junior hockey. He gave up hockey to pursue a career in basketball. In October 2000, the 7'1" 270-pound Mac-Cullough, a center for the NBA's Philadelphia 76ers, practiced with the NHL's Philadelphia Flyers. He wore custom-made size 19 skates.

4. ZDENO CHARA

The tallest player in NHL history was 6'9" Zdeno Chara. The Czech-born defenseman was a rookie for the New York Islanders in 1997.

5. TAFFY ABEL

Hall of Fame defenseman Clarence Abel was nick-named Taffy because of his fondness for saltwater taffy. Abel played for the New York Rangers and Chicago Black Hawks from 1926 to 1934. During that time his weight ballooned to as much as 260 pounds.

6. KJELL SAMUELSSON

Philadelphia Flyers defenseman Kjell Samuelsson played in the 1988 NHL All Star game. The big Swede was 6 feet 6 inches tall and weighed 235 pounds.

7. ERIC LINDROS

Eric Lindros is not only one of the best players in hockey he's also one of the biggest. The perennial All Star center stands 6 feet 5 inches and weighs 240 pounds.

8. BILL BENNETT

Bill Bennett played left wing for the Boston Bruins and Hartford Whalers from 1978 to 1980. The 6'5" 235-pound Bennett scored four goals during his 31-game NHL career.

9. **YIP FOSTER**

Harry "Yip" Foster was a defenseman who played for the Rangers, Bruins, and Red Wings from 1929 to 1935. The 6'6" Foster was the tallest player in the NHL at the time.

10. **PETE MAHOVLICH**

Pete Mahovlich played for Detroit, Montreal, and Pittsburgh between 1965 and 1981. He was the brother of superstar Frank Mahovlich. A good player in his own right, Pete scored 288 goals during his career. Despite being 6'5" tall, Pete was nicknamed "Little M," while his brother, who was five inches shorter, was known as "the Big M."

Mighty Atoms

Sometimes good things came in small packages. Right wing Theoren Fleury, although only 5 feet 6 inches tall, scored 51 goals for the Calgary Flames during the 1990–1991 season. It was said of 5'5" center Bobby Lalonde that "He'd be great in a short series." "Jumpin' Jake" Forbes, a 140-pound goalie, had an outstanding 1.96 goals against average while playing for the NHL's Hamilton Tigers in 1925. Tony "Mighty Mouse" Leswick was one of the most feared players in the league despite being one of the smallest.

1. **DICKIE BOON**

Dickie Boon was 5 feet 4 inches tall and weighed less than 120 pounds. Despite his tiny size, the defenseman was one of the greatest players of the pre–NHL era. A speed-skating champion, he was one of the first defensemen to rush the puck and poke-check opponents. Boon was elected to the Hockey Hall of Fame in 1952.

2. **RUSSELL BOWIE**

At 5 feet 6 inches and 122 pounds, Russell Bowie was an unlikely scoring champion. During his career, he averaged nearly three goals per game. His career was cut short in 1910 when he suffered a broken collarbone.

3. KEN DORATY

Ken Doraty was a 124-pound forward for the Toronto Maple Leafs. In a memorable six overtime game in the 1933 Stanley Cup semifinals against Boston, Doraty scored the game-winning goal in a 1-0 Toronto victory.

4. JOHN ROSS ROACH

John Ross Roach was nicknamed Little Napoleon. The 5'6", 130-pound goaltender for the New York Rangers recorded 13 shutouts and held opponents to a 1.41 goals against average during the 1928–1929 season.

5. ROY WORTERS

Roy "Shrimp" Worters was a 5'3" goalie who compiled a career 2.27 goals against average. His best season was 1928–1929, when he allowed only 1.15 goals per game while tending goal for the New York Americans. He won the Vezina Trophy as the NHL's best goalie in 1931.

6. AUREL JOLIAT

Left wing Aurel Joliat was nicknamed the Mighty Atom. Joliat played for the Montreal Canadiens from 1922 to 1938. Despite being only 5 feet 6 inches tall and weighing just 135 pounds, Joliat had a Hall of Fame career. Goaltender Tiny Thompson commented that Joliat's shot couldn't break a pane of glass, but it was so accurate that Joliat scored 270 goals during his NHL career.

7. KING CLANCY

King Clancy was known as "135 pounds of muscle and conversation." The trash-talking defenseman starred

for the Ottawa Senators and Toronto Maple Leafs during the 1920s and 1930s. In 1958, Clancy was in-
ducted into the Hockey Hall of Fame.

8. LARRY AURIE

Larry Aurie played for Detroit from 1927 to 1939. The
5'6", 139-pound right wing was nicknamed the Little
Rag Man. An All Star performer, Aurie scored 147
goals during his career.

9. MUSH MARCH

Mush March was known as the Mighty Midget. The 5'5"
right wing played for the Chicago Black Hawks from
1928 to 1945. He was so small that teammate Tuffy
Abel, one of the biggest players in the league, would
create a screen and let March shoot between his legs.
March scored 153 goals during his NHL career.

10. GEORGE HAINSWORTH

At 5'5", George Hainsworth was one of the shortest
goaltenders in NHL history. He was also one of the best.
His 1.91 career goals against average is the lowest in
NHL history. During the 1928–1929 season, the Montreal Canadiens' goalie had a record 22 shutouts.

Teenage Terrors

On March 21, 1923, 18-year-old King Clancy played all six positions for Ottawa in a 1-0 victory over Montreal. All of these players were hockey stars before they reached the age of 20.

1. WAYNE GRETZKY

As a 10-year-old, Wayne Gretzky scored 378 goals and 517 points in 85 games for a novice team in Brantford, Ontario. As an 18-year-old rookie with the Edmonton Oilers in 1979, Gretzky scored 51 goals and led the NHL in scoring with 137 points.

2. ARMAND GUIDOLIN

Armand "Bep" Guidolin, a left wing for the Boston Bruins, was 16 years old when he made his NHL debut on November 12, 1942, in a 3-1 loss to the Toronto Maple Leafs. Guidolin was the youngest player ever to appear in an NHL game. Guidolin scored 7 goals in his rookie season and 107 during his nine-year NHL career.

3. ALBERT FORREST

Seventeen-year-old Albert Forrest was the goaltender for the Dawson City Klondikes in the 1905 Stanley Cup challenge against the powerful Ottawa Silver Seven. In one game, Forrest surrendered 23 goals. It was said that he was the best player on the overmatched Dawson City team and the score would have been even more lopsided without his acrobatic saves. Humiliated by the loss, Forrest walked the last 350 miles back to Dawson City alone.

4. HARRY LUMLEY

Harry "Apple Cheeks" Lumley was the youngest goalie in NHL history. He was 17 when he made his debut with the Detroit Red Wings in 1943. Lumley played until 1960, winning 330 games and recording 71 shutouts.

5. TED KENNEDY

Ted Kennedy accomplished more as a teenager than most hockey players do in an entire career. The Toronto Maple Leafs' center made his NHL debut in 1944 at the age of 17. He scored 26 goals during his first full season. At the age of 19, Kennedy led the Maple Leafs to the Stanley Cup title. In Game 4 of the finals, he netted a hat trick. Kennedy went on to a Hall of Fame career in Detroit, and was a six-time All Star.

6. FRANK PATRICK

Frank Patrick was a star during the early years of the twentieth century. As an 18-year-old, he performed double duty as a player for the Montreal team and as a referee. On March 12, 1912, the defenseman set a record with a six-goal performance for Vancouver in a game against New Westminster.

7. DALE HAWERCHUK

Dale Hawerchuk was the youngest player to score 100 points in a season. The 18-year-old center for the Winnipeg Jets scored 103 points during the 1981–1982 season. He scored 518 goals and 1,409 points during his NHL career.

8. TOM BARRASSO

Tom Barrasso was 18 years old when he won the Vezina Trophy as the NHL's outstanding goaltender. The Buffalo Sabres' goalie had a 26-12-3 record during the 1982–1983 season.

9. BUSHER JACKSON

Harvey "Busher" Jackson was 18 years old when he joined the Toronto Maple Leafs in 1929. Jackson played on the famed Kid Line with Jim Primeau and Charlie Conacher. The left wing scored 241 goals in his NHL career. He was elected to the Hockey Hall of Fame in 1971.

10. DON GALLINGER

Center Don Gallinger was only 17 years old when he played his first NHL game with the Boston Bruins in 1942. His promising career ended prematurely in 1948 when he was suspended from the NHL for life for gambling.

Life Begins at 40

C onnie Madigan was 38 years old when the defenseman made his NHL debut with the St. Louis Blues
on February 6, 1973. All of the following players remained in the NHL until over the age of 40.

1. GORDIE HOWE

Detroit's Gordie Howe was 41 years old when he scored
a career-high 103 points during the 1968–1969 season. At age 48, Howe scored 102 points with the Houston Aeros of the World Hockey Association. He was 52
years old when he played his final NHL season with the
Hartford Whalers in 1980. In 1997, the 69-year-old
Howe played one shift for the Detroit Vipers in an International Hockey League (IHL) game.

2. MOE ROBERTS

On November 25, 1951, the Chicago Black Hawks
played the Detroit Red Wings. During the game, Chicago goalie Harry Lumley injured his knee. Moe Roberts, the team's 46-year-old trainer, volunteered to
finish the game. Roberts had made his NHL debut 26
years earlier and had not played in the league for 18

London Life-Portnoy/Hockey Hall of Fame

Gordie Howe was 52 when he played his last NHL season,
with the Hartford Whalers.

years. Roberts played surprisingly well, holding Detroit
scoreless in the third period at a 5-2 loss.

3. LESTER PATRICK

Game 2 of the 1928 Stanley Cup finals between the
New York Rangers and the Montreal Maroons had most
unlikely hero. During the first period, Rangers goaltender Lorne Chabot was knocked unconscious by a

shot and was unable to continue. In those days teams only carried one goaltender on their roster. The Rangers asked if they could use Alex Connell or Hughie McCormick, professional goaltenders who were seated in the stands, but the Maroons refused. Lester Patrick, the Rangers' 44-year-old coach, decided to take over as his team's goaltender. What made the substitution even more incredible was that Patrick had been a defenseman during his career as a player and had never appeared in an NHL game. Incredibly, Patrick made 18 saves in a 2-1 New York victory. It was his first and last game as a player in the NHL. With newly hired goaltender Joe Miller in the net, the Rangers won the Stanley Cup in five games.

4. JACQUES PLANTE

Toronto Maple Leafs goaltender Jacques Plante was 42 years old when he led the NHL with a 1.88 goals against average in 1971. Plante was 44 years old when he played his last NHL game with the Boston Bruins. Showing he was still as good as ever, he won seven of his last eight games, and had a goals against average of 2.00.

5. TIM HORTON

Tim Horton played 20 seasons with the Toronto Maple Leafs. The Hall of Fame defenseman was 42 years old when he was lured out of retirement by Buffalo's general manager Punch Imlach. Horton was good enough to be named the Sabres' Most Valuable Player. The 44-year-old Horton was still playing for Buffalo when he was killed in an automobile accident on February 21, 1974.

6. **DOUG HARVEY**

Another ageless defenseman was Doug Harvey. The seven-time Norris Trophy winner was 44 years old when he played his final season with the St. Louis Blues in 1969.

7. **JOHNNY BOWER**

In 1965, Toronto Maple Leafs goaltender Johnny Bower was 41 years old when he shared the Vezina Trophy with Terry Sawchuk. Bower was 43 years old when he helped his team win the Stanley Cup. He played in the NHL until he was 45 years old.

8. **JOHN BUCYK**

After playing his first two seasons with the Detroit Red Wings, Hall of Fame left wing John Bucyk starred for the Boston Bruins from 1958 to 1978. Bucyk was 43 years old when he retired.

9. **ALEX DELVECCHIO**

Alex Delvecchio played 24 seasons with the Detroit Red Wings. The center scored 456 goals and passed out 825 assists during his Hall of Fame career. Delvecchio played until he was 41 years old.

10. **ALLAN STANLEY**

Defenseman Allan Stanley was 41 years old in 1967 when he played on the Stanley Cup championship team, the Toronto Maple Leafs. Stanley was 43 years old when he finished his career with the Philadelphia Flyers.

Clothes Encounters

As a child, Guy Lafleur was so eager to get to the rink that he wore his uniform to bed. Another Montreal Canadien great, Howie Morenz, was such a clothes horse that he changed his clothes up to three times a day. Montreal winger Marcel Bonin borrowed Maurice Richard's glove in an attempt to break a slump and scored eight goals in eight games. Gary "Suitcase" Smith wore as many as 13 pairs of socks during a game. Montreal fans used to celebrate goals by throwing rubber boots on the ice.

1. EDDIE SHORE

Eddie Shore was a superhero on the ice and sometimes dressed the part. During the pregame warm-up, the Boston defenseman skated onto the ice wearing a cape, while the band played "Hail to the Chief." A valet removed the cape before the game began.

2. PADDY MORAN

Paddy Moran was a goaltender for the Quebec Bulldogs prior to the formation of the National Hockey League. Moran wore a baggy sweater that he claimed kept him warm in the drafty old arenas. The crafty Moran kept the sweater unbuttoned and would open it to catch shots. Moran was elected to the Hockey Hall of Fame in 1958.

3. CUMMY BURTON

The Detroit Red Wings and the Toronto Maple Leafs played in the 1956 Stanley Cup semifinals. Toronto fans were incensed when their star player, Tod Sloan, broke his shoulder in a collision with Detroit's Gordie Howe. Both Howe and Ted Lindsay received death threats. It was suggested that rookie Cummy Burton wear a Red Wings jersey with Lindsay's number 7 on the front and Howe's number 9 on the back. The idea was for Burton to skate onto the ice to see if anything happened. Wisely, Burton refused to be the guinea pig. Lindsay incited the Toronto crowd even more by scoring twice in Game 3. After scoring, Lindsay held his stick like a rifle and pretended he was shooting at the crowd.

4. KING CLANCY

St. Patrick's Day 1934 was King Clancy Day at Toronto's Maple Leaf Gardens. The popular defenseman was carried into the arena seated on a throne. Clancy was dressed in a robe and wore a silver crown befitting a king. He removed the robe revealing a green jersey with a shamrock on the front. As part of the tribute, floats were brought out onto the ice. Left wing Baldy Cotton popped out of a float shaped like a top hat and goaltender George Hainsworth emerged from one shaped like a boot. Clancy wore the green jersey throughout the first period of the game. The Maple Leafs defeated the New York Rangers 3 to 2.

5. CONN SMYTHE

The Maple Leaf Gardens in Toronto opened on November 12, 1931. A capacity crowd of 13,233 paid between $.95 and $2.75 to attend a game between the Maple Leafs and the Chicago Black Hawks. Maple Leafs owner Conn Smythe enforced a strict dress code. Many of the men in the crowd wore tuxedos and the women wore evening gowns. Smythe created the dress code to discourage the beer-drinking crowd. He promised that a lady could attend every game without fear of having her dress ruined by beer stains. Smythe was a snazzy dresser himself. In January 1937, Smythe wore an evening jacket, spats, and a top hat on the Maple Leafs bench during a game in Boston. Smythe said he was trying to bring a little class to Boston.

6. HARRY SMITH

On January 12, 1907, the Ottawa Silver Seven played the Montreal Wanderers. During the game, an Ottawa fan threw a large beaver hat on the ice with the Silver Seven's red, white, and blue colors. Ottawa forward Harry Smith picked up the hat and wore it throughout the game, which was won by Montreal.

7. WINNIPEG VICTORIAS

The 1902 Stanley Cup challenge matched the Winnipeg Victorias against the Toronto Wellingtons. During the warm-ups, the Victoria players wore gold dressing gowns over their uniforms. Despite their unorthodox outfits, Victoria won the Stanley Cup.

8. DOC ROMNES

Doc Romnes, a center for the Chicago Black Hawks, broke his nose during the 1938 season. To protect the injury, Romnes wore a Purdue University football helmet. Romnes led his team to the Stanley Cup championship.

9. AUREL JOLIAT

The Montreal Canadiens All Star left wing wore a black baseball cap during games. If his hat was knocked off, Joliat would stop chasing the puck in order to retrieve his cap. It was said that the only way to anger Joliat was to touch his hat.

10. HAT TRICK

In 1943, a Stetson dealer offered a new hat to any player who scored three goals in a game. The tradition of the hat trick was born. Whenever a player scores three goals, fans toss hats onto the ice.

Tools of the Trade

I n 1933, the Boston Bruins' Eddie Shore was the first player to wear a hockey helmet as protection because he feared retaliation from players and fans after seriously injuring Toronto's Ace Bailey during a game. Goalie Emile Francis introduced the trapper-style glove in 1948. Each of the players in this list had a memorable piece of equipment.

1. GERRY CHEEVERS

Gerry Cheevers was the goaltender for the great Boston Bruins team of the 1970s. The Hall of Fame goalie had a lifetime record of 230 wins, 102 losses, and 74 ties. Cheevers had black stitches painted on his mask where he would have been cut, had he not wore it.

2. CHUMNY HILL

The 1902 Stanley Cup challenge between the Toronto Wellingtons and Winnipeg Victorias produced several unusual moments involving the puck. In one game, the puck got stuck in the rafters of the arena. Action stopped while the players threw their sticks at the rafters to dislodge the puck. On another occasion, the puck split in half. Toronto's Chumny Hill shot half of the puck past the confused Victoria goalie for a goal.

3. ERNIE JOHNSON

Ernie Johnson was one of the best hockey players of the pre–NHL era. He used the longest stick in hockey history. Johnson often threw it at opposing players' feet to trip them. The long stick was finally banned in 1915. Johnson said the stick was buried following his retirement.

4. PETR KLIMA

Petr Klima broke his stick after every goal. He reasoned, "I have only one goal in each stick." Klima scored 312 goals in his NHL career that lasted from 1985 to 1997.

5. JACQUES LEMAIRE

Hall of Fame center Jacques Lemaire scored 366 goals for the Montreal Canadiens between 1967 and 1979. As a youth, Lemaire strengthened his shot by practicing hitting steel pucks instead of ones made of rubber.

6. WHITEY MERRITT

George "Whitey" Merritt was credited as the first goaltender to wear protective pads. On February 14, 1896, the Winnipeg goalie wore white cricket pads in a 2-0 victory against Montreal.

7. PAUL HENDERSON

Paul Henderson played right wing for the Detroit Red Wings, Toronto Maple Leafs, and Atlanta Flames between 1962 and 1980. He scored 236 goals in the NHL and another 140 goals during a five-year stint in the

WHA. In 1972, Henderson became a national hero when he scored the winning goals in three games as Canada defeated the Soviet Union in the Summit Series. During the 1966–1967 season, Henderson suffered from trachiatis, an inflammation of the breathing tube. To keep the cold rink air out of his lungs, Henderson wore a surgical mask during games.

8. MIKE GREEN

Mike Green was the referee of the 1905 Stanley Cup series between Ottawa and Rat Portage. Green wore the first helmet in hockey history to protect himself from the rough play.

9. JACK CRAWFORD

Jack Crawford was an All Star defenseman who played for the Boston Bruins from 1937 to 1950. Crawford was one of the first hockey players to wear a helmet. He wore the helmet because he was self-conscious about his bald head.

10. JIM HENRY

"Sugar Jim" Henry won 162 games during his NHL career as a goaltender from 1941 to 1955. Because Henry had a fear of getting varicose veins in his legs, he refused to tighten his goalie pads. Sometimes his pads would be turned around by a hard shot.

Dinky Rinks

Today, NHL games are played in modern arenas. Over the years, hockey has been played in all kinds of arenas.

1. KINGSTON HARBOR RINK

The first college hockey game was played between Queens' University and the Royal Military College. The game was played on an open-air rink in Kingston Harbor. There was a large bandstand in the middle of the ice. The bandstand blocked the view of the goaltenders who could not see the other goal. The game's winning goal was scored by Queens' University's Lennox Irving. The Royal Military College goalie was sitting on a snowbank strapping on a loose skate blade when Irving scored the uncontested goal.

2. MONTREAL ARENA

The Montreal Arena opened in 1898. It cost 35 cents for a reserved seat. For an extra dime, a fan could rent a fur rug to keep his or her legs warm in the drafty arena. The pipe and cigarette smoke was often so heavy that it was impossible to see the other end of the rink.

3. JOE LOUIS ARENA

On April 15, 1952, the Montreal Canadiens met the Detroit Red Wings in Game 4 of the Stanley Cup finals. Detroit led the series three games to none and had won seven playoff games in a row. Two fans, Pete and Jerry Cusimano, threw an octopus on the ice. Their father worked in the fish business. The eight tentacles of the octopus symbolized the eight games the Red Wings needed to win to be Stanley Cup champions. Detroit won the game 3-0 to sweep the series and a new tradition was born. Fans continue to throw octopuses on the ice at Red Wings games for good luck. At Detroit's Joe Louis Arena, a huge mechanical octopus was suspended from the rafters.

4. DEY'S ARENA

In the early years of the twentieth century, Ottawa fans watched hockey in Dey's Arena. Wind whistled through the cracks in the wooden boards and fans froze during the games. Mischievous fans used pea shooters to pelt opposing goalies whenever Ottawa players took a shot.

5. PHILADELPHIA SPECTRUM

During the 1967–1968 season, high winds blew off the roof of the new Philadelphia Spectrum, home of the Flyers. The hockey team was forced to play its remaining home games in Toronto and Quebec while the Spectrum's roof was being repaired.

6. WESTMOUNT ARENA

The Westmount Arena was the home of the Montreal Canadiens and Montreal Wanderers. The two teams were original members of the newly created National Hockey League. On January 2, 1918, the Westmount Arena burned down, destroying the equipment of both teams. The Canadiens moved to the Jubilee Arena and went on to become the most successful franchise in NHL history. By contrast, the financially strapped Wanderers dropped out of the league following the fire.

7. BUFFALO WAR MEMORIAL AUDITORIUM

Game 3 of the 1975 Stanley Cup finals between the Philadelphia Flyers and Buffalo Sabres was played in a fog worthy of a London evening. It was a warm, humid night in Buffalo and a fog developed inside the War Memorial Auditorium. The game was delayed 11 times as players waved towels in an attempt to clear the air. Buffalo won the game 3-2, but they lost the series to Philadelphia in six games.

8. WINNIPEG ARENA

Adverse ice conditions nearly postponed the 1902 Stanley Cup series between the Montreal AAAs and the Winnipeg Victorias. Sixty-degree temperatures melted the ice at the Winnipeg Arena. Fans sneaked into the arena by the hundreds through open windows. Players and officials attempted to mop up the water with towels. The game was played on a surface resembling slush more than ice. Montreal won the series two games to one.

9. MAPLE LEAF GARDENS

Toronto's Maple Leaf Gardens was one of hockey's most storied venues. In the early days of the gardens, there was a place on the concourse called "the Bull Ring." Bookmakers converged there to take bets on anything relating to the hockey game. One of the strangest wagers was betting on whether a male or female fan would be hit with the next puck clearing the boards.

10. BORDER CITIES ARENA

During the 1926–1927 season the Red Wings did not have a home arena in Detroit. The team played 22 games in the Border Cities Arena in Windsor, Ontario.

Centers of Attention

The center position has produced some of hockey's greatest scorers. Norm Ullman scored 490 goals during his career with the Detroit Red Wings and Toronto Maple Leafs. Gil Perreault of the Buffalo Sabres scored 512 goals and 1,326 points during his NHL career. Bryan Trottier found the net 524 times while starring for the New York Islanders and Pittsburgh Penguins. Ron Francis is one of the few players in NHL history to have 500 goals and 1,000 assists. From Howie Morenz to Wayne Gretzky, there have been many great centers in the NHL.

1. WAYNE GRETZKY

Wayne Gretzky was not only the greatest center in hockey history, he was also the best player who ever lived. Gretzky won 10 Art Ross trophies as the NHL scoring champion and nine Hart trophies as the league's Most Valuable Player. Gordie Howe said of Gretzky, "The only way to stop him is to lock him in the dressing room." The Great One set 62 NHL records. He holds the records for the most goals in a season (92), most assists in a season (163), and most points in a season (215). During the 1983–1984 season, he scored in a record 51 consecutive games. Gretzky

Paul Bereswill/Hockey Hall of Fame

Possibly the two greatest centers ever, Wayne Gretzky (right)
and Mario Lemieux (left), face off against each other in an
NHL All-Star game.

scored a record 894 goals and 2,857 points in his NHL
career. He has more assists (1,963) than any other
player has points.

2. MARIO LEMIEUX

Bobby Orr called Mario Lemieux the most talented
player in NHL history. Super Mario scored three minutes into his first NHL game and has never stopped.

Lemieux has overcome Hodgkin's disease and back injuries to become one of the game's greatest scorers. He won six scoring titles and was voted the NHL's Most Valuable Player three times. Despite missing several years because of illness and injury, Lemieux has scored more than 600 goals. In his greatest season, 1988–1989, the Pittsburgh Penguins' center scored 85 goals and 199 points.

3. PHIL ESPOSITO

Phil Esposito's motto was "If at first you don't succeed, shoot, shoot again." Esposito scored 717 goals, the fourth most in NHL history. He would park near the crease and pounce on rebounds. During the 1970–1971 season, the Boston Bruins' center scored 76 goals, 18 more than Bobby Hull's single-season record. Esposito won five Ross trophies and two Hart trophies.

4. JEAN BELIVEAU

Jean Beliveau led the Montreal Canadiens to ten Stanley Cup champions. Twice he won the Hart Trophy and he was the NHL's leading scorer during the 1955–1956 season. A great passer and playmaker, Beliveau was the ultimate team player. During his career, he had 507 goals and 712 assists.

5. MARK MESSIER

Mark Messier played on six Stanley Cup championship teams. Six times he scored more than 100 points in a season. Twice Messier won the Hart Trophy as the league's Most Valuable Player. Messier has scored more than 650 goals and 1,100 assists.

6. STEVE YZERMAN

Steve Yzerman has starred with the Detroit Red Wings since 1983. He has scored more than 600 goals and

1,000 assists during his career. Five times he scored 50 or more goals in a season. During the 1988–1989 season, Yzerman scored 65 goals and 155 points.

7. MARCEL DIONNE

Marcel Dionne was one of the most prolific scorers in NHL history. His 731 career goals ranks third, behind Wayne Gretzky and Gordie Howe. The Los Angeles Kings' royal center led the NHL in scoring with 137 points during the 1979–1980 season.

8. STAN MIKITA

Stan Mikita played for the Chicago Black Hawks from 1959 to 1980. Mikita scored 541 goals and 926 assists during his career. In 1967, Mikita won the Ross, Hart, and Byng trophies. He also won four Ross trophies and two Hart trophies during his career.

9. HOWIE MORENZ

Howie Morenz was voted the greatest player of the first half of the twentieth century. He was such a fast skater that one goalie said his number 7 looked like 777. The Montreal Canadiens' center won three Hart and two Ross trophies. Morenz played on three Stanley Cup championship teams.

10. BOBBY CLARKE

Punch Imlach said of Bobby Clarke, "He gives more of himself than anybody I've seen." The tenacious Clarke was the leader of the Broad Street Bullies, the great Philadelphia Flyers teams of the 1970s. Clarke won three Hart trophies and played on two Stanley Cup championship teams.

The Right Stuff

S ome of the greatest players in NHL history have played right wing. Yvan Cournoyer of the Montreal Canadiens scored 428 goals and played in six NHL All Star games. Bill Cook, who played with the New York Rangers from 1926 to 1937, was considered the best right wing prior to Maurice Richard.

1. GORDIE HOWE

No hockey player played as well for as long as Gordie Howe of the Detroit Red Wings. The man known as Mr. Hockey was a 21-time All Star and won six Hart trophies and six Ross trophies. Howe scored 801 goals and 1,850 points in 26 NHL seasons.

2. MAURICE RICHARD

Maurice "the Rocket" Richard was called, "The Babe Ruth of Hockey." He terrorized goalies during his career with the Montreal Canadiens, which lasted from 1942 to 1960. Hall of Fame goalie Glenn Hall recalled, "When he came flying toward you with the puck on his stick, his eyes were lit up. Flashing and gleaming like a pinball machine. It was terrifying." Richard was the first player to score 50 goals in a season and 500 goals in a career. It was once said that the only way to stop Richard was to shoot him.

3. GUY LAFLEUR

Guy Lafleur was another great Montreal Canadien right winger. Unpredictable and elusive, Lafleur was very difficult to defend. Lafleur won three Ross and two Hart trophies. Between 1974 and 1980, Lafleur scored 50 or more goals every year.

4. BRETT HULL

Like his father, Bobby, Brett Hull is one of the greatest goal scorers in NHL history. The Golden Brett has scored more than 650 goals. Three times he scored more than 70 goals in a season. During the 1990–1991 season, the St. Louis Blues right winger scored 86 goals.

5. JARI KURRI

Jari Kurri was one of the primary offensive weapons of the great Edmonton Oilers teams of the 1980s. He scored 601 goals during his career and played on five Stanley Cup championship teams. A clutch performer, four times Kurri led all scorers in the Stanley Cup playoffs. Kurri scored 71 goals during the 1984–1985 season.

6. MIKE BOSSY

Few players have been as consistent as Mike Bossy of the New York Islanders. Bossy scored 50 or more goals for nine consecutive seasons. Five times he scored 60 or more goals. His 83 assists during the 1981–1982 season was a record for a right winger. Although he only played 10 seasons, Bossy scored 573 goals.

7. MIKE GARTNER

Mike Gartner scored 708 goals during his career that lasted from 1979 to 1998. Gartner starred for the Washington Capitals, Minnesota North Stars, New York Rangers, Toronto Maple Leafs, and Phoenix Coyotes. Seven times Gartner topped the 40-goal mark in a season. He played in seven NHL All Star games.

8. BERNIE GEOFFRION

Bernie "Boom Boom" Geoffrion played in 11 NHL All Star games between 1952 and 1963. The possessor of one of hockey's hardest shots, Geoffrion scored 393 goals. One of the first players to score 50 goals in a season, Geoffrion won two Ross trophies as the league's leading scorer.

9. JAROMIR JAGR

One of the best Europeans ever to play in the NHL, Jaromir Jagr is a two-time Ross Trophy winner. The big Czech set a record for right wingers when he had 87 assists for the Pittsburgh Penguins during the 1995–1996 season. Jagr also scored 62 goals during that season. He scored 127 points during the 1998–1999 season.

10. CHARLIE CONACHER

Charlie Conacher was one of the NHL's first great scorers. The Big Bomber led the league in goals scored five times between 1931 and 1936. The Toronto Maple Leafs' star right winger was part of the famed Kid Line. Conacher won the Ross Trophy in 1934 and 1935.

The Left Stuff

The left-winger position has never been as high scoring as their right-winger counterparts. While Gordie Howe and Maurice Richard received the attention, there have been plenty of great left wingers who have played in the NHL.

1. BOBBY HULL

Bobby Hull was one of hockey's most charismatic players. The Golden Jet was one of the fastest skaters and hardest shooters in the game. Hull won three Ross and two Hart trophies. Seven times he led the NHL in goals scored and he played 12 All Star games. Hull scored 610 goals in the NHL and 303 more in the WHA.

2. FRANK MAHOVLICH

Frank Mahovlich starred at left wing for the Toronto Maple Leafs, Detroit Red Wings, and Montreal Canadiens. The Big M played in 15 NHL All Star games between 1959 and 1974. Mahovlich scored 533 goals and played on six Stanley Cup championship teams.

3. TED LINDSAY

Ted Lindsay played in 11 NHL All Star games. Terrible Ted played on four Stanley Cup winners with the Detroit Red Wings. One of the toughest players in NHL history, Lindsay scored 379 goals.

4. LUC ROBITAILLE

On January 18, 2002, Luc Robitaille of the Detroit Red Wings scored his 611th goal, breaking Bobby Hull's record for career goals for left-wingers. During the 1992–1993 season, Robitaille, then playing for the Los Angeles Kings, set season records for left wingers with 63 goals and 125 points.

5. JOHN BUCYK

John Bucyk was not as heralded as his teammates Bobby Orr and Phil Esposito, but he was no less important to the Boston Bruins' championship teams of the early 1970s. Bucyk played 22 of his 24 NHL seasons in Boston. He scored 556 goals and had 813 assists.

6. MICHEL GOULET

Michel Goulet played in five NHL All Star games. The left winger scored 548 goals during his career with the Quebec Nordiques and Chicago Black Hawks. He scored more than 50 goals for four consecutive seasons from 1983 to 1986.

7. AUREL JOLIAT

Aurel Joliat led the Montreal Canadiens to three Stanley Cup championships. One of the great scorers in the NHL during the 1920s and 1930s, he netted 270 goals.

He won the Hart Trophy in 1934 as the league's Most Valuable Player.

8. CY DENNENY

Cy Denneny was a scoring machine during the early years of the National Hockey League. Denneny scored 246 goals in 326 games, giving him the third highest goals-per-game average in NHL history, behind only Mario Lemieux and Mike Bossy. The Ottawa Senators' left winger played on five Stanley Cup championship teams.

9. DICKIE MOORE

A six-time All Star, Dickie Moore played on six Stanley Cup championship teams. Moore scored 261 goals during his career that lasted from 1951 to 1968. He was the league's leading scorer with Montreal in 1958 and 1959.

10. BOB GAINEY

Bob Gainey was probably the best defensive forward in NHL history. He won four Frank Selke trophies as the league's best defensive forward. The Hall of Fame left winger played on five Stanley Cup championship teams in Montreal.

For the Defense

There have been many great defensemen. Chris Chelios has won the Norris Trophy three times. Earl Seibert was a 10-time All Star. Brian Leetch scored 102 points and won the Norris Trophy in 1992.

1. BOBBY ORR

Bobby Clarke said of Bobby Orr, "Orr was actually too good for the rest of us in the NHL." The Boston Bruins' defenseman revolutionized his position. Before Bobby Orr, no defenseman had ever scored 100 points in a season. Orr accomplished the feat six years in a row. Twice Orr led the NHL in scoring and three times he was the league's Most Valuable Player. During the 1970–1971 season, Orr had moves never seen on the ice. The only thing that could stop him was bad knees, which shortened his career.

2. RAY BOURQUE

Ray Bourque joined the Boston Bruins in 1979, a year after Bobby Orr retired. Unlike Orr, Bourque would have a long career. When he retired in 2001, Bourque had 410 career goals and 1,169 assists. Bourque played in 19 All Star games and won the Norris Trophy five times. His greatest strength was that he had no weakness. He was a superb passer, excellent shooter, and sterling defender.

3. PAUL COFFEY

Paul Coffey was a defenseman with incredible offensive skills. During the 1985–1986 season, the Edmonton Oilers' star set a single-season record for defensemen with 48 goals. That season Coffey scored 138 points, one point less than Bobby Orr's record. Coffey won three Norris trophies and played on four Stanley Cup championship teams. Coffey finished his career with 396 goals and 1,531 points.

4. DOUG HARVEY

Doug Harvey won seven Norris trophies and played in 13 NHL All Star games. He was a master of stealing the puck and one of the best defensive players ever to take the ice. Harvey played on six Stanley Cup championship teams with the Montreal Canadiens.

5. DENIS POTVIN

In 1987, Denis Potvin became the first NHL defenseman to score 1,000 points in a career. Potvin played on four Stanley Cup championship teams with the New York Islanders. A great checker and excellent passer, Potvin won three Norris trophies.

6. EDDIE SHORE

Eddie Shore was the greatest defenseman of his day. The Boston Bruins' defenseman won the Hart Trophy in 1933, 1935, 1936, and 1938. His rough play made him a hated man throughout the league. Sportswriter

Ring Lardner called him "The only man in hockey generally known to the people who dislike hockey."

7. **RED KELLY**

Red Kelly led defensemen in goals eight times. He played in 13 All Star games between 1950 and 1963. Kelly won the Norris Trophy as a member of the Detroit Red Wings in 1954, and he played on eight Stanley Cup championship teams.

8. **BRAD PARK**

Brad Park played in nine consecutive NHL All Star games from 1970 to 1979. Overshadowed by Bobby Orr, Park starred for the New York Rangers and Boston Bruins. Although he never won the Norris Trophy, he finished second in the voting six times.

9. **PIERRE PILOTE**

Pierre Pilote won the Norris Trophy in 1963, 1964, and 1965. Pilote was an eight-time All Star with the Chicago Black Hawks. Blessed with superb all-around skills, Pilote was elected to the Hockey Hall of Fame.

10. **LARRY ROBINSON**

Larry Robinson played on six Stanley Cup championship teams with the Montreal Canadiens. Robinson won the Norris Trophy in 1977 and 1980. He scored 958 points during his NHL career.

The Puck Stops Here

Lorne Chabot recorded 73 shutouts and had a 2.04 goals against average. Hap Holmes is the only goaltender to play for Stanley Cup champions on four different teams: the 1914 Toronto Blueshirts, the 1917 Seattle Metropolitans, the 1918 Toronto Arenas, and the 1925 Victoria Cougars. Boston Bruins goalie Gerry Cheevers had a career record of 230 wins, 102 losses, and 74 ties. Bernie Parente of the Philadelphia Flyers won two Vezina trophies and won 47 games during the 1973–1974 season. Turk Broda won four Stanley Cup championships with the Toronto Maple Leafs and had a 1.98 career-playoff goals against average.

1. JACQUES PLANTE

Jacques Plante described the plight of the goalie as "How would you like it in your job if every time you made a mistake, a red light went on over your desk and fifteen thousand people stood up and yelled at you?" Plante won seven Vezina trophies and played on six Stanley Cup championship games. The innovative Plante was the first goalie to leave the crease and the first to regularly wear a mask. He won 434 games and had 82 shutouts. Nine times between 1956 and 1971 he led the NHL in goals against average.

2. TERRY SAWCHUK

Terry Sawchuk had a record 103 shutouts during his NHL career. Between 1951 and 1955 Sawchuk allowed less than two goals a game for five consecutive years. He won four Vezina trophies and played on four Stanley Cup championship games. Sawchuk won 447 games during his NHL career despite a long list of serious injuries, which included a severed wrist tendon that prevented him from closing his hand, elbow surgery that left his right arm two inches shorter than his left, and more than 400 stitches in his face. The eccentric Sawchuk insisted on keeping teeth he had knocked out during games, bone spurs removed from his elbow, and he even preserved his removed appendix.

3. KEN DRYDEN

Ken Dryden won six Stanley Cup championships in seven NHL seasons. The five-time Vezina Trophy winner never lost more than 10 games in a season. The Montreal Canadien goaltender won 258 games, lost 57, and tied 74 and had a career 2.24 goals against average.

4. GLENN HALL

Glenn Hall popularized the butterfly style in which he dropped to his knees, forming an inverted V. Known as Mr. Goalie, Hall won 407 games and recorded 84 shutouts during his NHL career. The 13-time All Star won three Vezina trophies. Hall played an incredible 532 consecutive games for the Chicago Black Hawks between 1955 and 1962. Despite his success, Hall hated being a goaltender. He was so upset that he vomited before each game. "I hate every minute I play," Hall admitted.

5. GEORGE HAINSWORTH

In the history of the NHL, no goalie was harder to score on than George Hainsworth. He had 94 shutouts and had a career goals against average of 1.91. During the 1928–1929 season the Montreal Canadiens' goalie gave up only 43 goals in 44 games and recorded 22 shutouts. Hainsworth was a three-time Vezina Trophy winner.

6. PATRICK ROY

On December 26, 2001, Colorado's Patrick Roy became the first NHL goalie to win 500 games. Roy recorded his 59th shutout with a 2-0 victory against Dallas. A clutch goalie, Roy won the Smythe Trophy in 1986, 1993, and 2001.

7. BILL DURNAN

The career of Bill Durnan had several similarities with that of Ken Dryden. Both goaltenders played all seven years of their NHL career with the Montreal Canadiens. Each man won six Vezina trophies as the league's top goalie. Durnan set a record with a 309-minute stretch, the equivalent of more than five games, without allowing a goal. Durnan won 208 games, lost 112, and tied 62 with a 2.36 career goals against average.

8. DOMINIK HASEK

Dominik Hasek won the Hart Trophy as the NHL's Most Valuable Player in 1997 and 1998. The Dominator has won the Vezina Trophy five times. He had 13 shutouts while playing goaltender for the Buffalo Sabres during the 1997–1998 season. Hasek won a gold medal with the Czechoslovakian Olympic team in 1998.

9. ALEX CONNELL

Alex Connell played goaltender in the NHL from 1924 to 1937. Twice Connell had 15 shutouts in a season and 81 in his career. He had four consecutive seasons in which his goals against average was less than 1.50. His 1.91 career goals against average is tied with George Hainsworth for the best in NHL history.

10. TONY ESPOSITO

Tony Esposito was known as Tony O because of his ability to shut out the opposition. During the 1969–1970 season, the Chicago Black Hawks' goalie had a league-high 15 shutouts. Esposito won 423 games and had 76 shutouts during his career. He won the Vezina Trophy in 1970, 1972, and 1974.

Sizzling Slap Shots

Right winger Lanny McDonald scored 500 goals with his blistering shot. Left winger Frank Mahovlich used his powerful slap shot to score 533 goals. Goaltender Jacques Plante said that defenseman Tim Horton had the hardest slap shot in the league. Ray Bourque was another defenseman who had a tremendous shot from the point. These players were hockey's hardest shooters.

1. BOBBY HULL

Bobby Hull's slap shot was once measured at 140 miles per hour. Hall of Fame goaltender Jacques Plante said of Hull's shot, "You had to see it coming to believe it." Once, Plante's arm was paralyzed for five minutes after being struck by a Hull shot. Pittsburgh Penguins goalie Les Binkley described what it was like to face Hull's shot: "It starts off looking like a sweet pea and then disappears altogether." During a 1967 program warm-up, one of Hull's shots sailed over the glass and hit Toronto Maple Leafs owner Harold Ballard in the face, breaking his nose in four places. Hull used his feared slap shot to score 610 goals and led the league in goals seven times.

2. REGGIE LEACH

Reggie Leach scored 381 goals during his NHL career. During the 1975–1976 season, the Philadelphia Flyers' right wing led the league with 61 goals. Leach's slap shot was measured at more than 115 miles per hour. His nickname was the Riverton Rifle.

3. ANDY BATHGATE

Andy Bathgate intimidated goaltenders with his slap shot. Bathgate scored 349 goals during his career that lasted from 1953 to 1971. His high shot was so hard that some goalies ducked. One of his slap shots struck Montreal goaltender Jacques Plante in the face, opening a cut. The injury caused Plante to become the first goaltender to wear a mask.

4. BERNIE GEOFFRION

Bernie Geoffrion was nicknamed Boom Boom because of his booming slap shot. The Montreal Canadiens' right winger blasted the puck past goalies 393 times during his career and twice led the league in goals scored.

5. BRETT HULL

Like his father, Bobby, Brett Hull has one of hockey's hardest shots. Brett has scored more than his Hall of Fame father with a quick release and a 100-miles-per-hour shot. During a three-year period from 1989 to 1992, Brett scored 228 goals.

6. CHARLIE CONACHER

Charlie Conacher had the hardest shot of the pre–slap shot era. The Big Bomber injured several goaltenders

Dave Sandford/Hockey Hall of Fame

Brett Hull unleashes one of his powerful slap shots, which blisters
past goalies at speeds approaching 100 miles per hour.

with his powerful shots. Five times he led the NHL in
goals scored and had a five-goal game against Hall of
Fame goaltender Roy Worters in a January 19, 1932,
game.

7. DIDIER PITRE

Didier Pitre was nicknamed Cannonball because his
shot seemed like it was fired out of a cannon. In 1914,

chicken wire was installed at the ends of Victoria's rink to protect spectators from Pitre's blasts. He scored 30 goals during the 1914–1915 season, half of the goals the Montreal Canadiens scored that season.

8. CECIL DYE

Cecil "Babe" Dye had hockey's hardest shot in the 1920s. Dye was the first to break the protective glass in Toronto's Mutual Street Arena with a shot. The Hall of Famer led the NHL in goals scored in 1921, 1923, and 1925.

9. GUY LAFLEUR

Guy Lafleur had the reputation of being one of the hardest shooters of the 1970s. The Montreal Canadiens' right winger had six consecutive 50-goal seasons and won three NHL scoring titles. The season before he joined the Canadiens, Lafleur scored 130 goals for the Quebec Ramparts.

10. AL MacINNIS

Defenseman Al MacInnis had a slap shot few forwards could match. MacInnis won the Smythe Trophy in 1989 when he led all scorers in playoff points and led the Calgary Flames to the Stanley Cup title. The next season he scored 103 points.

Roadrunners

Boston Bruins right winger Rick Middleton was nick-named Nifty because of his sensational skating ability. Early hockey star Cyclone Taylor could skate through an entire team and once scored a goal skating backward. Defenseman Earl Seibert had unmatched acceleration. These skaters could really fly.

1. BOBBY HULL

Bobby Hull was nicknamed the Golden Jet because of his ability to outskate defenders. Hull was once timed at nearly 30 miles per hour. His breakaway speed led to many scoring opportunities.

2. JACK BRANNEN

Jack Brannen played center and rover for the Montreal Shamrocks at the turn of the twentieth century. The fastest skater in hockey, Brannen was the world champion speed skater in the 220-yard distance in 1900.

3. JACK LAVIOLETTE

Jack Laviolette was hockey's original Flying French-man. Known as the Speed Merchant, the French Cana-

dian star played defenseman and winger for the
Montreal Canadiens. His hockey career as a player
ended in 1919 when he lost a foot in an automobile
race. He was elected to the Hockey Hall of Fame in
1962.

4. HOWIE MORENZ

Howie Morenz was so fast that he had several nicknames: the Stratford Streak, Mitchell Meteor, Canadian
Comet, and Hurtling Habitant. Morenz was regarded as
the greatest player of his day and was a three-time winner of the Hart Trophy. His career ended when he broke
his leg in a game on January 28, 1937.

5. MIKE GARTNER

Mike Gartner won several "Fastest Man in Hockey"
skating contests. The speedy right winger scored 708
goals during his NHL career and played in seven All
Star games.

6. PAUL COFFEY

Paul Coffey was one of the best skaters ever to play
hockey. The high scoring Edmonton defenseman had
tremendous acceleration as well as superb agility. His
burst of speed allowed him to cover both ends of the
ice.

7. YVAN COURNOYER

Nicknamed the Roadrunner because of his brilliant
speed, Yvan Cournoyer was able to elude bigger defenders. The 5'7" right winger scored 428 goals during
his career with the Montreal Canadiens. Chicago goaltender Tony Esposito remarked, "He seemed to appear
from nowhere." Like the cartoon character from which

he got his nickname, it seemed no one ever caught Cournoyer.

8. PAVEL BURE

Pavel Bure may have been the fastest skater of the 1990s. The Russian Rocket scored 60 goals while playing for the Vancouver Canucks during the 1993 and 1994 seasons.

9. BILL MOSIENKO

In 1950, Chicago Black Hawks Bill Mosienko won a speed-skating contest of NHL players. Three years later, a poll of sportswriters voted him the fastest skater in hockey. The Hall of Fame right winger played in five NHL All-Star games.

10. HEC KILREA

Hec Kilrea was known as the Hurricane because of his fast skating. Kilrea set a record in an NHL speed-skating contest. The left winger played in the NHL from 1925 to 1940.

Check, Please

Right wing Punch "Old Elbow" Broadbent was known for his backchecking. Center Frank Boucher was one of the game's best poke-checkers. Left wing Woody Dumart was renown for his close-checking skill. Defensemen Red Horner was a great body-checker. Check out some of hockey's best checkers.

1. GILLES MAROTTE

Gilles Marotte was nicknamed Captain Crunch because of his hard-hitting style. The 200-pound defenseman was one of the best body-checkers of the 1960s and 1970s.

2. JOHN BUCYK

Bobby Orr said he never saw anyone hit harder than teammate John Bucyk. The 215-pound left wing was one of hockey's hardest checkers. He was particularly adept at the hip check.

3. TIM HORTON

John Ferguson, one of the NHL's most feared enforcers, said that he never saw anyone check harder than Toronto defenseman Tim Horton. "He hits with tremendous force," Ferguson recalled. One of the strongest men in hockey, Horton could crush a man in his powerful bear hug.

4.   JACK STEWART

"Black Jack" Stewart was one of the hardest body-checkers in NHL history. Detroit Red Wings teammate Sid Abel said Stewart had an arm like a cement wall. The Hall of Fame defenseman played in four consecutive NHL All Star games between 1947 and 1950.

5.   BILL BARILKO

Bill Barilko was nicknamed Bashin' Bill because of his brutal body checks. Barilko was notorious for his snake hips. The Toronto Maple Leafs' defenseman played five seasons in the NHL. He was only 24 years old when he was killed in an airplane crash on August 26, 1951.

6.   MARCEL PRONOVOST

Marcel Pronovost played for the Detroit Red Wings and Toronto Maple Leafs between 1949 and 1970. The Hall of Fame defenseman was one of the game's best poke-checkers. He was known to throw his body into checks with reckless abandon.

7.   ERNIE JOHNSON

Ernie Johnson was one of the best players of the first decade of the twentieth century. Johnson had the longest reach in hockey and used the longest sticks. He used these assets to become one of hockey's first great poke-checkers.

8.   FRANK NIGHBOR

The player credited with popularizing the poke check was Frank Nighbor. The Flying Dutchman was famed for his brilliant stickhandling ability. The Hall of Fame center won the Hart Trophy in 1924.

9.   LEO BOIVIN

Leo Boivin was considered the best body-checker of the 1950s and 1960s. Built like a fireplug, Boivin could deliver a devastating hip check. One of hockey's toughest defensemen, Boivin was elected to the Hockey Hall of Fame in 1986.

10.   BILL QUACKENBUSH

Bill Quackenbush was the least penalized defenseman in NHL history. He rarely body-checked an opposing player, but he was one of the best poke-checkers in the league. Quackenbush's specialty was breaking up the rush with his stick checks.

The Best Years of Their Lives

During the 1928–1929 season, Boston Bruins goaltender Tiny Thompson had a 1.15 goals against average. Philadelphia Flyers goalie Bernie Parente won a record 47 games during the 1973–1974 season. In 1966, Bobby Hull of the Chicago Black Hawks became the first NHL player to score more than 50 goals in a season. Here are 10 more unforgettable seasons.

1. WAYNE GRETZKY

Wayne Gretzky had so many great seasons, it's difficult to choose one. During the 1985–1986 season, the Edmonton Oilers' center set NHL records with 163 assists and 215 points. Perhaps his best season was 1981–1982 when he scored a record 92 goals. His 212 points broke his previous NHL record by 48 points.

2. BOBBY ORR

Bobby Orr led the NHL with 87 assists and 120 points during the 1969–1970 season. The Boston Bruins' defenseman won the scoring title, finishing 21 points ahead of runner-up Phil Esposito. The amazing Orr won the Hart, Ross, Norris, and Smythe trophies.

3. MARIO LEMIEUX

Wayne Gretzky is the only player to score 200 points in a season, but Mario Lemieux came within one point of reaching the milestone during his 1988–1989 season.

Paul Bereswill/Hockey Hall of Fame

Mario Lemieux slips through two New York Islander defenders as he makes his way toward the goal.

The 23-year-old Pittsburgh Penguins star scored 76 goals and 123 assists. His 199 points were 31 more than his rival, Wayne Gretzky.

4. GEORGE HAINSWORTH

It's unlikely a goaltender will ever match the records of George Hainsworth during the 1928–1929 season. The Montreal goalie recorded 22 shutouts and had a goals against average of 0.92. Hainsworth shut out the opposition in half of the games he played.

5. JOE MALONE

During the 1917–1918 season, Montreal's Joe Malone scored 44 goals in 20 games. His record of goals in a season was not broken for 27 years. Malone's 2.2 goals per game has never been approached. A player today would have to score 176 goals in a season to match his pace.

6. PHIL ESPOSITO

Phil Esposito scored 76 goals and 76 assists during the 1970–1971 season. His 76 goals were 18 more than Bobby Hull's previous record and the 152 points he scored broke his own NHL record by 26. Esposito took 550 shots, 136 more than Bobby Hull's record.

7. BRETT HULL

Brett Hull of the St. Louis Blues scored 86 goals during the 1990–1991 season. Only Wayne Gretzky ever scored more goals in a season. His 86 goals were 35 more than the runner-up that season, the largest margin ever for a goal leader.

8. STAN MIKITA

During the 1966–1967 season, Chicago Black Hawks Stan Mikita became the first player to win the Hart,

Ross, and Byng Trophy in one year. Mikita became the first player to reach 60 assists in a season and his 97 points tied Bobby Hull's NHL single-season record.

9. **PAUL COFFEY**

Paul Coffey set a record for goals by a defenseman with 48 during the 1985–1986 season. Coffey also passed out 90 assists to his high-scoring Edmonton team-mates. He had a streak of 28 consecutive games in which he scored a point.

10. **MAURICE RICHARD**

Maurice Richard became the first player to score 50 goals during the 1944–1945 season. Richard scored 50 goals in 50 games. His season goal record was not broken for 21 years. It would be 36 years before another player matched Richard's mark of 50 goals in 50 games.

Great Games

During the 1920–1921 season, Ottawa left winger Cy Denneny scored six goals in a 12-5 victory against Hamilton. Montreal's Maurice Richard scored all five goals in a 5-1 victory over Toronto in Game 2 of the 1944 Stanley Cup playoff series. Detroit goaltender Norm Smith held the Montreal Maroons scoreless in a six overtime 1-0 win in the 1936 Stanley Cup semifinals. Here are some more of hockey's greatest performances.

1. FRANK McGEE

On January 16, 1905, Frank McGee of the Ottawa Silver Seven scored 14 goals in a 23-2 rout of Dawson City in the Stanley Cup challenge series. McGee averaged nearly three goals in a game during his career.

2. JOE MALONE

Joe Malone of the Quebec Bulldogs scored seven goals in a 10-6 victory over the Toronto St. Patricks on January 31, 1920. An eighth goal was waived off because of an offside. Malone had scored 39 goals in 24 games during the NHL regular season.

3. **DARRYL SITTLER**

Toronto Maple Leafs center Darryl Sittler set an NHL record by scoring 10 points in an 11-4 win against the Boston Bruins on February 7, 1976. Sittler scored six goals and had four assists. Maple Leafs owner Harold Ballard presented Sittler with a silver tea service to commemorate his achievement.

4. **MARIO LEMIEUX**

In a game against the New Jersey Devils played on December 31, 1988, Pittsburgh Penguins Mario Lemieux accomplished something no other player has done. Lemieux scored five different types of goals. He scored on a power play, at even strength, shorthanded, by penalty shot, and an open net goal. Lemieux had five goals and three assists in Pittsburgh's 8-to-6 victory.

5. **LORNE CHABOT**

Toronto Maple Leafs goaltender Lorne Chabot shut out Boston 1-0 in Game 5 of the 1933 Stanley Cup semifinal series. What makes the feat extraordinary is that the game lasted six overtimes, the equivalent of three regulation games.

6. **BILL MOSIENKO**

Bill Mosienko of the Chicago Black Hawks scored the fastest hat trick in NHL history. On March 21, 1952, Mosienko scored three goals during a 21-second span during the third period of a game against the New York Rangers. Gus Bodnar assisted on all three goals. A fourth shot seconds later hit the post. The Black Hawks overcame a 6-2 deficit and rallied for a 7-6 victory.

7.   IAN TURNBULL

Toronto's Ian Turnbull set a record for defensemen when he scored five goals in a 9-1 victory against Detroit on February 22, 1977. The outburst broke a personal slump for Turnbull. Prior to his five-goal game, he had not scored a goal in 30 games.

8.   RED BERENSON

Gordon "Red" Berenson of the St. Louis Blues scored six goals in an 8-0 victory against the Philadelphia Flyers on November 7, 1968. The Red Baron became the first player in NHL history to score six goals in a road game. Four of Berenson's goals came in the second period.

9.   PAUL COFFEY

Paul Coffey was a defenseman who scored like a center. On March 14, 1986, the Edmonton Oilers star scored eight points in a game against Detroit. Coffey scored two goals and had six assists.

10.   PATRIK SUNDSTROM

Patrik Sundstrom had the game of his life in the April 22, 1988, Stanley Cup second-round playoff game against the Washington Capitals. The New Jersey Devils' center scored three goals and had five assists in a 10-4 victory. Sundstrom scored only 15 goals during the regular season.

Lopsided Losses

O n March 30, 1944, the Montreal Canadiens routed the Toronto Maple Leafs 11-0 during the Stanley Cup semifinal series. During the opening round of the 1987 Stanley Cup playoffs, Jari Kurri scored four goals and Wayne Gretzky had six assists as the Edmonton Oilers embarrassed the Los Angeles Kings 13 to 3. Phil Esposito scored four goals as the Boston Bruins blanked the Toronto Maple Leafs 10-0 in Game 1 of the 1969 Stanley Cup quarterfinal series. After a humiliating 11-to-1 loss to Detroit, Montreal goaltender Patrick Roy demanded to be traded because he felt coach Mario Tremblay left him in the game too long. Four days later, Roy was shipped to Colorado. This list features hockey's most one-sided games.

1. **1949 DENMARK WORLD TEAM**
The 1949 World Hockey Championships marked Denmark's first appearance in the tournament. The Danes were immediately thrown to the wolves—the Sudbury Wolves. The team from Canada crushed the Danes 47 to 0. The game was the worst defeat in the history of the World Hockey championships.

2.   1944 MIDDLEBURY COLLEGE

Cornell was a college hockey powerhouse when the team played Middlebury College in a 1944 game. Cornell overwhelmed outmanned Middlebury 30 to 0. Cornell's Dick Rondeau scored 12 goals and had 11 assists in the massacre.

3.   1905 DAWSON CITY KLONDIKES

The biggest rout in Stanley Cup history occurred on January 16, 1905. The Ottawa Silver Seven, the best team of the time, destroyed the Dawson City Klondikes 23 to 2. Ottawa outscored Dawson City 32 to 4 to sweep the best-of-three series.

4.   1944 NEW YORK RANGERS

On January 23, 1944, the Detroit Red Wings blanked the New York Rangers 15 to 0 in the most lopsided game in NHL history. The Red Wings outshot the Rangers 58 to 9. Detroit scored eight goals in the third period. Syd Howe scored a hat trick and Joe Carveth had four assists.

5.   1910 OTTAWA

In a game during the 1910–1911 season, the star-studded Renfrew Kings crushed Ottawa 17 to 2. Renfrew owner M. J. O'Brien encouraged the rout by offering $100 to his players for each goal scored. Cyclone Taylor scored one goal while skating backward. Taylor explained that the reason he did the showboat move was because the Ottawa fans had pelted him with lemons and whiskey bottles during the previous game.

6.   1920 QUEBEC BULLDOGS

The Montreal Canadiens outscored the Quebec Bulldogs 16-3 in a game played on March 3, 1920. It was the most goals scored in an NHL game.

7. **1981 WINNIPEG JETS**

On November 11, 1981, the Minnesota North Stars defeated the Winnipeg Jets 15 to 2. The North Stars scored eight goals in the second period. Minnesota center Bobby Smith scored four goals and had seven points.

8. **1957 NEW YORK RANGERS**

Brian Collins and Syd Smith had hat tricks as the Toronto Maple Leafs trounced the New York Rangers 14 to 1 in a game played on March 16, 1957. Center Ted Kennedy had four assists for the Maple Leafs.

9. **1993 SAN JOSE SHARKS**

The Calgary Flames annihilated the San Jose Sharks 13 to 1 in a February 10, 1993, game. Calgary's Jeff Reese set a record for goaltenders with three assists.

10. **1975 WASHINGTON CAPITALS**

The 1975 Washington Capitals were one of hockey's worst teams, while the Philadelphia Flyers were one of the best. Their game on December 21, 1975, figured to be a mismatch—and it was. Rick Martin scored four goals as the Flyers crushed the Capitals 14 to 2.

Terrible Teams

The 1953–1954 Chicago Black Hawks had the worst record of the 1950s in the NHL. Chicago had a 12-51-7 record during that dismal season. Believe it or not, there have been worse teams.

1. 1974–1975 WASHINGTON CAPITALS

The 1974–1975 Washington Capitals set records for futility. Washington had a record of 8-67-5. The hapless Capitals lost a record 17 games in a row during one stretch. They had a 37-game winless streak on the road. The team lost three games by 10 or more goals. The defense surrendered a record 446 goals. The Capitals were so bad that the team had three different head coaches during the year: Jim Anderson, Red Sullivan, and Milt Schmidt.

2. 1930–1931 PHILADELPHIA QUAKERS

The 1929–1930 Pittsburgh Pirates had a 5-36-5 record. The struggling franchise was moved to Philadelphia and the name was changed to the Quakers. Their name may have changed, but the results were the same. The Quakers finished the season with a record of 4-36-4. The team was owned by the former world lightweight boxing champion, Benny Leonard. The Quakers disbanded the following season.

3. 1943–1944 NEW YORK RANGERS

The New York Rangers' teams of the World War II years were dreadful. The 1942–1943 Rangers had a 25-game winless streak. The next year they were even worse. New York began the season with a 15-game winless streak and finished the year with a 6-39-5 record. The defense allowed more than six goals a game. The team was so bad that Lester Patrick considered suspending operations until World War II was over.

4. 1928–1929 CHICAGO BLACK HAWKS

The 1928–1929 Chicago Black Hawks scored only 33 goals in the 44-game season. Because Chicago Stadium was not yet finished, the Black Hawks played most of their home games in Fort Erie. Chicago had a 15-game winless streak and finished the season with a 7-29-8 record.

5. 1919–1920 QUEBEC BULLDOGS

The Quebec Bulldogs lasted for only one season in the NHL. The 1919–1920 team was one of the worst in league history. Quebec had a 4-20-0 record and allowed a record 7.4 goals per game.

6. 1980–1981 WINNIPEG JETS

The 1980–1981 Winnipeg Jets had a record 30-game winless streak. During the streak the Jets lost 23 games and tied 7. Their record for the season was 9-57-14.

7. **1992–1993 OTTAWA SENATORS**

The Ottawa Senators played their first NHL season in 1992–1993. The Senators had a 38-game winless streak on the road. Ottawa's record for the year was 10-70-4.

8. **1989–1990 QUEBEC NORDIQUES**

The 1989–1990 Nordiques had a record of 12-61-7. Many of their losses were by lopsided scores. A joke about the Nordiques circulated around the league: "How many Nordiques does it take to change a tire? Only one, but they'll all be there if it's a blowout."

9. **1972–1973 NEW YORK ISLANDERS**

The New York Islanders played their first NHL season in 1972. The expansion Islanders had one streak in which they were 1-20-1 on the road. New York had a 12-60-6 record for the season.

10. **1992–1993 SAN JOSE SHARKS**

The 1992–1993 Ottawa Senators won only 10 games, but the San Jose Sharks were not much better. The Sharks' record that year was 11-71-2.

Seasons They'd Rather Forget

Even superstars have subpar seasons. In his final season, high scoring defenseman Paul Coffey scored only two goals in the 1997–98 season. Bryan Trottier, who scored 524 goals in his career, managed only 4 in the 1993–1994 season. Stan Mikita had only 8 goals in his rookie season, but scored 533 more during his career.

1. **MARK MESSIER**

Few would have guessed from Mark Messier's 1978–1979 season with the Cincinnati Stingers of the WHA that he would score more than 600 goals in the NHL. Messier scored only 1 goal in 47 games that season. Three seasons later with the Edmonton Oilers, Messier had his first 50-goal season.

2. **PATRICK ROY**

Patrick Roy is the only goaltender in NHL history to win 500 games. His minor league record was less than stellar. In 1982–1983 with the Granby Bisons, Roy had an abysmal 13-35-1 record with an astronomic 6.26 goals against average. Two years later, Roy was 16-25-1 with a 5.55 goals against average.

Dave Sandford/Hockey Hall of Fame

His abysmal minor league record notwithstanding,
Patrick Roy would go on to become one of the
NHL's most successful goalkeepers.

3. GORDIE HOWE

As an NHL rookie, Gordie Howe scored 7 goals in 58
games for the Detroit Red Wings during the 1946–1947
season. By the time he retired in 1980, Gordie Howe
scored 801 goals in the NHL.

4. PHIL ESPOSITO

Chicago Black Hawks rookie Phil Esposito scored 3
goals and 2 assists in 27 games during the 1963–1964

season. Esposito scored 717 goals during his Hall of Fame career.

5. JOE MALONE

Joe Malone led the NHL with 44 goals in 20 games during the 1917–1918 season. Five years later, Malone scored 1 goal in 20 games with the Montreal Canadiens. After not scoring a point the following season, Malone retired.

6. ANDY BATHGATE

In his rookie season, Bathgate scored zero goals in 18 games with the 1953 New York Rangers. The hard-shooting Bathgate won the Ross Trophy in 1962 and was later elected to the Hockey Hall of Fame.

7. JARI KURRI

Jari Kurri scored 71 goals with the Edmonton Oilers during the 1984–1985 season. The next year he led the NHL with 68 goals. In his final season, Kurri scored only 5 goals in 70 games with the Colorado Avalanche. When he retired in 1998, Kurri had scored 601 goals.

8. BERNIE GEOFFRION

Bernie "Boom Boom" Geoffrion twice led the NHL in goals scored. After spending most of his career with the Montreal Canadiens, Geoffrion finished his career in 1968 with the New York Rangers. In his final season, he scored only five goals in 59 games.

9. MARCEL DIONNE

Marcel Dionne ranks third in NHL history in goals scored with 731. Dionne scored 7 goals in his final NHL season with the 1988–1989 New York Rangers.

10. **TONY ESPOSITO**

Hall of Fame goaltender Tony Esposito won 423 games in his NHL career. His best season was the 1969–1970 season, when the Chicago Black Hawks' goalie had a 38-17-8 record with 15 shutouts and a 2.17 goals against average. His worst season was 1981–1982 when Esposito struggled to a 19-25-8 record with a poor 4.52 goals against average.

The Offense Rests

L eft wing Willie Brussert played in the NHL from 1970 to 1976 and scored one goal in 129 games. Right winger Billy Cameron played in 39 games in the NHL between 1923 and 1926 and did not score a point. Patsy Callighen played in 36 games for the 1927 New York Rangers and was held scoreless. Meet some of the least offensive players in hockey history.

1. GUYLE FIELDER

Center Guyle Fielder played professional hockey from 1947 to 1973. Fielder scored more than 600 goals in various leagues. He had brief stints in the NHL with the 1950–1951 Chicago Black Hawks and the 1957–1958 Detroit Red Wings. In nine NHL games, Fielder was unable to score a single point.

2. OLIVER REINIKKA

Oliver Reinikka played center and right wing for the New York Rangers during the 1926–1927 season. Reinikka was born in Canada of Finnish heritage. A press agent gave Reinikka the nickname Ollie Rocco, hoping it would make him popular with the Italian population of New York City. Reinikka played in 16 games, but did not score a point.

3. BILL MIKKELSON

Bill Mikkelson was a defenseman who played for the Los Angeles Kings, New York Islanders, and Washington Capitals between 1971 and 1977. He scored only 4 goals in 147 games. During the 1974–1975 season with Washington, Mikkelson had a minus 82 rating, the worst in NHL history. The rating indicated that the opposing team scored 82 more goals than the Capitals while Mikkelson was on the ice.

4. PAUL McINTOSH

Paul McIntosh played for the Buffalo Sabres from 1974 to 1976. In 48 games the defenseman did not score a goal. McIntosh had an incentive clause in his 1975 contract that he would receive $15,000 if he played in 40 games. Late in the season, McIntosh was within 1 game of receiving the bonus. Buffalo Floyd Smith was instructed by general manager Punch Imlach not to put McIntosh in the game. A few of the Sabres' players took things into their own hands and tossed McIntosh over the boards onto the ice so he would receive his bonus.

5. KIM CLACKSON

Defenseman Kim Clackson played for the Pittsburgh Penguins and Quebec Nordiques from 1979 to 1981. Clackson did not score a goal in 100 NHL games. He did spend 320 minutes in the penalty box.

6. LARRY MELNYK

It took Larry Melnyk five years to score his first NHL goal. Melnyk was a rookie defenseman with the Boston

Bruins in 1980. He did not score a goal until five years later with the Edmonton Oilers. Melnyk was so surprised that he said, "I didn't even know it went in."

7. DON SPRING

Defenseman Don Spring was not exactly the second coming of Bobby Orr. He played for the Winnipeg Jets from 1990 to 1994. In 259 NHL games, Spring scored just one goal.

8. MILT HALLIDAY

Left wing Milt Halliday played for the Ottawa Senators from 1926 to 1929. Halliday scored just one goal in 67 games during his NHL career.

9. GORD STRATE

Gord Strate played for the Detroit Red Wings from 1956 to 1959. Strate was never compared with teammate Gordie Howe as a scoring threat. He played in 61 games and did not score a point.

10. MARTY HOWE

Marty Howe was the son of hockey great Gordie Howe. He played for the Hartford Whalers and Boston Bruins from 1979 to 1985. Howe scored 2 goals in six NHL seasons, 799 fewer than his famous father.

net Losses

On March 19, 1981, Toronto Maple Leafs goalie Michel Larocque allowed nine goals in the second period of a 14-4 loss to the Buffalo Sabres. Gordon Scott, a goalie with the Quebec Nordiques from 1989 to 1991, had a career 2-16-0 record and a 5.80 goals against average. When these goaltenders were in the net, the defense rested.

1. STEVE BUZINSKI

The 1942–1943 New York Rangers, decimated by the loss of players going to war, needed a goaltender in the worst way, and got one. Steve Buzinski had played minor league hockey with the Swift Current Indians, but had no NHL experience. Although he may have lacked ability, he certainly did not lack confidence. He said that catching pucks was "as easy as picking cherries off a tree." Buzinski was such a bad goalie that he was given the nickname the Puck Goesinski. His career record was 2-6-1 with a 5.89 goals against average.

2. TUBBY McAULEY

Ken "Tubby" McAuley was another dreadful goaltender with the New York Rangers during World War II.

McAuley had a 17-64-15 record for the Rangers from 1943 to 1945 with a 5.61 goals against average. In his first game, McAuley gave up 15 goals to the Toronto Maple Leafs. He gave up his first goal 15 seconds into the game. During his rookie season, he had a dismal 6-39-5 record with a 6.24 goals against average. On January 21, 1945, McAuley surrendered 4 goals in 80 seconds in a 14-3 loss to the Boston Bruins.

3. DAVE REECE

Boston Bruins goaltender Dave Reece was nicknamed the Human Sieve. In his 14th and last NHL game, he gave up six goals and a record-breaking 10 points to Toronto's Darryl Sittler in an 11-4 loss on February 7, 1976.

4. JIM STEWART

Boston Bruins goalie Jim Stewart's NHL career was brief, but memorable. On January 10, 1980, Stewart played his only NHL game, a 7-4 loss to the St. Louis Blues. He played one period, giving up five goals while recording only four saves.

5. LORNE ANDERSON

Lorne Anderson played three games in goal for the 1952 New York Rangers. On March 23, 1952, he played his third and last game, a 7-6 loss to the Chicago Black Hawks. Anderson gave up three goals in 21 seconds to Chicago's Bill Mosienko, the fastest hat trick in NHL history. Anderson blew a four-goal lead late in the third period.

6. IVAN MITCHELL

Ivan Mitchell played in only 22 NHL games for the Toronto St. Patricks between 1919 and 1922. Only eight times in NHL history has a player scored six or more goals in a game and Mitchell was in the net for two of them. On January 10, 1920, Newsy Lalonde of Montreal scored six goals against Mitchell in a 14-7 Canadiens' victory. Three weeks later, Mitchell gave up seven goals to Joe Malone in a 10-6 loss to the Quebec Bulldogs.

7. HOWARD LOCKHART

Howard Lockhart had a 16-41-0 record while playing for Toronto, Quebec, Hamilton, and Boston from 1919 to 1925. On February 16, 1921, Lockhart gave up five goals to Newsy Lalonde in a 10-5 loss to the Montreal Canadiens. The hapless Hamilton goalie surrendered six goals to Corb Denneny in a 10-3 loss to the Toronto St. Patricks on January 26, 1921. That same year, on March 7, Corb's brother Cy also scored six goals in a game against Lockhart, a 12-5 victory for the Ottawa Senators.

8. MICHEL BELHUMEUR

Michel Belhumeur played for the Washington Capitals for two seasons and never won a game. During the 1974–1975 season, Belhumeur had a 0-24-3 record and a 5.36 goals against average. The following season, he was 0-5-1 with a 5.09 goals against average.

9. FRANK BROPHY

Frank Brophy was 3-18-0 in the net for the 1919–1920 Quebec Bulldogs. His career goals against average of 7.11 was one of the worst in NHL history.

10. MIKE SANDS

Mike Sands played in six NHL games for the Minnesota North Stars from 1984 to 1987. His record was 0-5-0 and his career goals against average was 5.17.

Who's Minding the net?

Occasionally, a player other than a goaltender is forced into action as goalie. Usually the substitution is because of an injury to the regular goaltender. Harry Mummery, who played six years as a defenseman in the NHL, had a 2-1-0 record as goaltender with a high 6.28 goals against average. On February 28, 1941, Andy Branigan, a defenseman for the New York Americans, replaced injured goaltender Chuck Rayner and held Detroit scoreless for seven minutes in a 5-4 victory.

1. RED HORNER AND ALEX LEVINSKY

Toronto Maple Leafs All Star defenseman Red Horner replaced goaltender Lorne Chabot when he was penalized during a March 15, 1932, game against the Detroit Red Wings. Horner gave up one goal in his one-minute stint as a goalie. Another defenseman, Alex Levinsky, was given a chance as goaltender for a minute of Chabot's penalty. He too allowed one goal in one minute. Detroit won the game 6 to 2.

2. ALBERT LEDUC

When Montreal goaltender George Hainsworth was whistled for a two-minute penalty in a December 2, 1931, game against Chicago, Albert "Battleship" Leduc was brought in to mind the net. Leduc gave up one goal in two minutes in a 2-1 loss to the Black Hawks.

3. KING CLANCY

Hall of Fame defenseman King Clancy had two brief stints as a goaltender. On December 27, 1924, Clancy replaced penalized Ottawa Senators goaltender Alex Connell and held Toronto scoreless for two minutes in a 4-3 victory. On March 15, 1932, while playing for the Toronto Maple Leafs, Clancy was placed in goal while goaltender Lorne Chabot spent time in the penalty box. Like his teammates Red Horner and Alex Levinsky, Clancy gave up one goal in one minute.

4. ROGER JENKINS

New York Americans defenseman Roger Jenkins replaced injured goaltender Earl Robertson in the second period of a game against the New York Rangers, played on March 18, 1939. Jenkins allowed seven goals in 30 minutes of an 11-5 loss.

5. AL SHIELDS

Defenseman Al Shields twice replaced injured New York Americans Roy Worters during the 1931–1932 season. Shields appeared in a 3-0 loss to the New York Rangers on November 17, 1931, and in an 11-3 defeat to the Toronto Maple Leafs on January 19, 1932. Shields gave up nine goals in 41 minutes as goaltender.

6. CHARLIE CONACHER

Hall of Fame right winger Charlie Conacher had four short stints as goaltender and never allowed a goal. On November 20, 1932, he replaced penalized Maple Leafs goaltender Lorne Chabot for two minutes in a 7-0 loss to the New York Rangers. The Big Bomber again replaced a penalized Lorne Chabot on March 16, 1933, in a 1-0 loss to Detroit. On March 16, 1935, Conacher replaced injured George Hainsworth in the net of a 5-3 win against the Montreal Canadiens. As a member of the Detroit Red Wings, Conacher replaced injured goalie Tiny Thompson in a 7-3 loss to the New York Rangers on February 21, 1939.

7. CHARLIE SANDS

Montreal center Charlie Sands replaced injured goaltender Wilf Cude in the second period of a February 22, 1940, game against the Chicago Black Hawks. Sands allowed five goals in 25 minutes as Chicago routed Montreal 10 to 1.

8. ODIE CLEGHORN

Odie Cleghorn, the playing coach of the Pittsburgh Pirates, played one game in goal. On February 23, 1926, Cleghorn gave up only two goals in a 3 to 2 victory over the Montreal Canadiens.

9. SPRAGUE CLEGHORN

Sprague Cleghorn, brother of Odie, had two brief stints as a goaltender. The Ottawa defenseman replaced penalized Clint Benedict in a 4-3 victory against Toronto, played on February 18, 1919. As a defenseman for the Montreal Canadiens he replaced penalized Georges Vezina in a 4-2 loss to Ottawa on February 1, 1922.

Cleghorn did not give up a goal in his two games in the net.

10. HUGH PLAXTON

Montreal Maroons left winger Hugh Plaxton replaced Flat Walsh in the first period of a November 22, 1932, game against the New York Americans. Plaxton yielded five goals in 57 minutes in a 5-2 loss.

One-Game Wonders

L arry "King" Kwong scored 363 goals during his minor league career, but he was held scoreless in his one game with the New York Rangers. Defenseman Bill Anderson played 10 seasons in the minor leagues before playing in one playoff game for the Boston Bruins in 1943. All of these players appeared in just one NHL game.

1. DON CHERRY

Don Cherry said, "When I was a kid, I prayed for enough talent to be a pro hockey player, but I forgot to say NHL, because they only gave me enough to make the minors." Cherry played 18 years in the minors, but only one game in the NHL. Cherry played defenseman in a 1955 playoff game for the Boston Bruins, but he went on to become an outstanding coach with the Bruins in the 1970s.

2. ALEX WOOD

Goaltender Alex Wood played professional hockey from 1928 to 1945. The Scotsman played only one game in the NHL for the New York Americans. He was goaltender in a 3-2 loss to the Montreal Maroons on January 31, 1937. Trailing 8-0 in one minor league game, Wood was again facing a forward on a break-away. Wood shocked the player by stepping aside and saying, "Be my guest." The befuddled player hesitated for a second, then fired the puck into the empty net.

3. DOUG McKAY

Left winger Doug McKay is the only player to play in his only NHL game in a Stanley Cup final for a winning team. McKay did not score in his appearance with the Detroit Red Wings in the 1950 Stanley Cup finals against the New York Rangers.

4. JASON HERTER

Jason Herter, the eighth overall pick in the 1989 NHL entry draft, played in only one NHL game. The defense-man scored an assist in his only game for the New York Islanders during the 1995 season.

5. BILL CHALMERS

Bill Chalmers scored more than 450 goals during his professional hockey career. Chalmers was the leading scorer in the IHL in 1960 and the league's Most Valuable Player in 1965. The center did not score in his only NHL game with the 1954 New York Rangers.

6. GORD HAIDY

Right winger Gord Haidy scored more than 430 goals during his professional career that lasted from 1944 to 1964. Haidy played in only one NHL game, a Stanley Cup playoff game for the Detroit Red Wings in 1950.

7. ROLLY HUARD

Rolly Huard played in only one NHL game, but he made the most of it. He played for the Toronto Maple Leafs as an emergency injury replacement in a game played on December 14, 1930. Huard scored a goal in the game, but was never given another chance to play in the NHL.

8. LEN BRODERICK

Goaltender Len Broderick was loaned to the Toronto Marlboros of the Ontario Hockey Association (OHA) to the Montreal Canadiens for one game to replace injured goalie Jacques Plante. In his only NHL appearance, Broderick played well as Montreal defeated the Toronto Maple Leafs 6 to 2 in a game played on October 30, 1957.

9. JIM McBURNEY

Three times Jim McBurney led minor leagues in goals scored. McBurney played in one NHL game for the 1953 Chicago Black Hawks. Although he did not score a goal, he was credited with an assist.

10. GALEN HEAD

Right winger Galen Head played in one game with the 1967 Detroit Red Wings. The next season he led the Eastern Hockey League (EHL) in goals scored with 67 while playing for the Johnstown Jets.

Unlikely Heroes

Sometimes hockey heroes came from unexpected sources.

1. MEL HILL

Going in to the 1939 Stanley Cup playoffs, Boston Bruins right winger Mel Hill had scored only 12 NHL goals. In the 1939 Stanley Cup finals against the New York Rangers, Hill scored 3 game-winning overtime goals, including the series winner in Game 7. The heroics earned Hill the nickname Sudden Death.

2. MUD BRUNETEAU

Right winger Mud Bruneteau scored two goals during his rookie season with the Detroit Red Wings. On March 24, 1936, the rookie scored the game-winning goal in the longest game in NHL history. Bruneteau's goal in the sixth overtime gave Detroit a 1-0 victory against the Montreal Maroons.

3. ALFIE MOORE

Goaltender Alfie Moore had a 7-14-0 record during his NHL career. Although he had not played in the NHL during the season, Moore was the goaltender for the Chicago Black Hawks during Game 1 of the Stanley Cup finals on April 5, 1938. Moore, who had played for the Pittsburgh Hornets of the American Hockey League, was brought up to replace Black Hawks goalie Mike Karakas, who had suffered a broken toe. Moore did not disappoint as he held the Toronto Maple Leafs to one goal in a 3-1 victory. After the game, NHL president Frank Calder declared that Moore was ineligible for the remainder of the series because he was not under contract with the Black Hawks.

4.   BILL BARILKO

Bill Barilko scored only 26 goals during his five-year NHL career. On April 21, 1951, Barilko scored an over-time goal to give the Toronto Maple Leafs a 3-2 victory over the Montreal Canadiens in the fifth and deciding game of the Stanley Cup finals.

5.   HARDY ASTROM

The Montreal Canadiens' record 28-game unbeaten streak came to an end on February 23, 1978, in a 6-3 loss to the New York Rangers. The unlikely hero was Rangers goalie Hardy Astrom, who was playing in his first NHL game. Astrom's career record in the NHL was 17-44-12.

6.   LES CUNNINGHAM

Les Cunningham scored only 26 points during his NHL career. On January 28, 1940, the Chicago Black Hawks' center tied a league record when he scored 5 points in one period. Cunningham scored two goals and had three assists in the third period of an 8-1 victory against the Montreal Canadiens.

7. ERIC DESJARDINS

On June 3, 1993, Eric Desjardins of the Montreal Canadiens became the only defenseman to score a hat trick in a Stanley Cup game. Desjardins had scored only 13 goals during the regular season.

8. AL HILL

In his first NHL game on February 14, 1977, Philadelphia Flyers center Al Hill scored five points in a 6-4 victory over the St. Louis Blues. Hill's five-point game was the greatest offensive debut in NHL history. Hill scored 2 goals and had three assists. Hill scored only 40 goals during his eight-year NHL career.

9. CHRIS KONTOS

Los Angeles Kings forward Chris Kontos scored only two goals during the 1988–1989 season. During the Stanley Cup playoffs, Kontos scored nine goals in 11 games. He had six power play goals in the series against the Edmonton Oilers, won by the Kings in 7 games.

10. PETE BABANDO

Left winger Pete Babando scored only six goals during the 1949–1950 season. On April 23, 1950, Babando scored the game-winning goal in overtime in the seventh game of the Stanley Cup, lifting the Detroit Red Wings to a 4-3 victory over the New York Rangers.

Their Cups Runneth Over

Jacques Plante, Larry Robinson, Frank Mahovlich, Bryan Trottier, Dickie Moore, and "Boom Boom" Geoffrion are among the players who have been on six Stanley Cup championship teams. Each of the players included in this list played on at least six Stanley Cup championship teams.

1. HENRI RICHARD

Center Henri Richard played on 11 Stanley Cup championship teams as a member of the Montreal Canadiens between 1956 and 1973. The only time the Canadiens lost the Stanley Cup final with Richard on the team was in 1967 against the Toronto Maple Leafs.

2. JEAN BELIVEAU

Jean Beliveau was another Montreal Canadiens center who frequently raised the Stanley Cup in victory. Beliveau retired in 1971, following his 10th Stanley Cup championship.

3. YVAN COURNOYER

Montreal right winger Yvan Cournoyer also played on 10 Stanley Cup championship teams. Cournoyer played on Cup winners in 1965, 1968, 1969, 1971, 1973, 1976, 1977, 1978, and 1979.

4. CLAUDE PROVOST

Right winger Claude Provost was another Montreal Canadiens player who had the good fortune to play on many championship teams. Provost was a member of nine Stanley Cup championship teams between 1956 and 1969.

5. RED KELLY

Red Kelly played on eight Stanley Cup championship teams. What makes his success remarkable is that he never played on the Montreal Canadiens. Four of Kelly's cups were with the Detroit Red Wings in the 1950s and the other four in the 1960s with the Toronto Maple Leafs.

6. MAURICE RICHARD

Maurice Richard retired in 1960 with eight Stanley Cup championships. The Montreal Canadiens' superstar won Stanley Cups in his final five seasons.

7. JACQUES LEMAIRE

Montreal center Jacques Lemaire played in a Stanley Cup championship in his first season in 1968 and closed out his career on a Cup winner in 1979. Lemaire played on eight Stanley Cup championship teams in 12 NHL seasons.

8. SERGE SAVARD

Defenseman Serge Savard was a member of seven Stanley Cup championship teams in Montreal. This included a stretch of four straight titles in the late 1970s.

9. KEN DRYDEN

Hall of Fame goaltender Ken Dryden played in seven NHL seasons and six times he was on Stanley Cup championship teams. Dryden was one of the main reasons for Montreal's success during the period. His career playoff record was 80 wins and 32 losses.

10. MARK MESSIER

Mark Messier scored 109 goals in Stanley Cup playoff games. The explosive scoring center won five Stanley Cup championships with the Edmonton Oilers and one with the New York Rangers.

Dave Sandford/Hockey Hall of Fame

Shown on the ice for the New York Rangers,
Mark Messier won a total of six Stanley Cups with the
Rangers and the Edmonton Oilers.

They Never Won the Stanley Cup

In 2001, Colorado Avalanche defenseman Roy Bourque finally won his first Stanley Cup in his 22nd season. Newsy Lalonde, Doug Bentley, Chuck Rayner, and Peter Stastny are among the great players who never played on a Stanley Cup championship team.

1. MARCEL DIONNE

When Marcel Dionne retired in 1990 as the third highest scorer in NHL history, he had played 18 seasons with the Detroit Red Wings, Los Angeles Kings, and the New York Rangers. Dionne not only never played on a Stanley Cup championship team, he never even played in a final or semifinal series.

2. JEAN RATELLE

Jean Ratelle was a Hall of Fame center who scored 491 goals during his 21 NHL series. Ratelle never played on a Stanley Cup championship team. He played in the Stanley Cup finals with the New York Rangers in 1972 and with the Boston Bruins in 1977 and 1978, but came away without the Cup each time. "I'd trade almost everything for one Stanley Cup," Ratelle lamented.

3. BRAD PARK

Defenseman Brad Park played for the New York Rangers, Boston Bruins, and Detroit Red Wings. The nine-time All Star defenseman played 17 seasons in the NHL without ever being on a Stanley Cup championship team.

4. GIL PERREAULT

Gil Perreault played for the Buffalo Sabres from 1970 to 1987. The Hall of Fame center scored 512 goals, but he never played on a Stanley Cup championship team.

5. MIKE GARTNER

Mike Gartner is one of the handful of players to score more than 700 goals. He played 19 seasons in the NHL, without ever being on a Stanley Cup winning team. Gartner played for the Washington Capitals, Minnesota North Stars, New York Rangers, Toronto Maple Leafs, and the Phoenix Coyotes.

6. DARRYL SITTLER

Darryl Sittler was another star who suffered frustration in the Stanley Cup playoffs. Sittler played with the Toronto Maple Leafs, Philadelphia Flyers, and the Detroit Red Wings during his 15-year career. He scored 484 goals, but he never played on a Stanley Cup championship team.

7. NORM ULLMAN

Hall of Fame center Norm Ullman divided his career between the Detroit Red Wings and Toronto Maple

Leafs. The 11-time All Star scored 490 goals in his 20-year career. Despite the achievements, Ullman never played on a Stanley Cup championship team.

8. DALE HUNTER

Center Dale Hunter holds a record he'd rather do without. During his 19-year career with the Quebec Nordiques, Washington Capitals, and the Colorado Avalanche, Hunter played in more Stanley Cup games without winning the Cup than any player in NHL history.

9. GUY CHARRON

Guy Charron played 12 seasons in the NHL with the Montreal Canadiens, Detroit Red Wings, Kansas City Scouts, and Washington Capitals. The center played in 734 regular-season games, but never played in a single Stanley Cup playoff game.

10. HARRY HOWELL

Defenseman Harry Howell played 21 seasons in the National Hockey League. The Hall of Fame defense-man played most of his career on the New York Rangers during their long Stanley Cup drought. The seven-time All Star never played in a Stanley Cup finals.

Stanley Cup Curiosities

The Stanley Cup cost less than $50 when it was purchased in 1893 by Frederick Arthur Stanley, governor-general of Canada. The Cup's original name was the Dominion Challenge Cup, but it was later named for Lord Stanley. Ironically, Lord Stanley returned to England and never attended a Stanley Cup game. Over the years the Stanley Cup has been stolen, left by the side of the road, and used as a flowerpot.

1. 1905 OTTAWA SILVER SEVEN

The Ottawa Silver Seven won the Stanley Cup in 1905. During a night of drunken celebration, some of the Ottawa players kicked the Stanley Cup onto the frozen Rideau Canal and left it there. When they came to their senses the next morning, they raced back to the canal and found the cup where they had left it.

2. 1924 MONTREAL CANADIENS

The Montreal Canadiens won the Stanley Cup in 1924. Canadiens owner Leo Dandurand threw a party to celebrate the team's victory. On the way to the party, the automobile transporting some of the players had a flat tire. The players changed the flat, but inexplicably left the Stanley Cup by the side of the road. Luckily, when they returned, the Stanley Cup was still there.

3. 1907 MONTREAL WANDERERS

When the Montreal Wanderers won the Stanley Cup in 1907, they took it to a photographer's studio. While at the studio, a young man stole the trophy, hoping to hold it for ransom. No one seemed to care, so he returned the trophy. When the Montreal team returned to retrieve their trophy they found geraniums planted in it.

4. MARK WEGGONER

The Colorado Avalanche won the 2001 Stanley Cup. On August 22, 2001, Mark Weggoner, vice president of finance for the corporation that owns the team, climbed to the top of Mount Elbert with the 35-pound Stanley Cup strapped to his back. The 14,233-foot peak is the highest mountain in Colorado.

5. KEN KILANDER

The Montreal Canadiens won five consecutive Stanley Cups from 1956 to 1960. When it became apparent that the Chicago Black Hawks were going to end the Canadiens' streak in 1961, it was more than one Montreal fan could stand. Ken Kilander broke the glass and stole the trophy from the lobby at Chicago Stadium. After he was apprehended, Kilander told the judge he was taking the Stanley Cup back to Montreal where it belonged.

6. HARRY SMITH

The Montreal Wanderers won the Stanley Cup in 1906. The players asked to see the Stanley Cup, but no one seemed to know where it was. Finally, Ottawa player Harry Smith remembered that he had it at home in his closet.

7. DICKIE BOON

In the early days of the Stanley Cup competition, not everyone treated it with reverence. Dickie Boon, captain of the 1903 Montreal AAA team, said, "The Cup is far from beneficial to the game, it is detrimental." Boon felt the Stanley Cup playoffs were too long.

8. THOMAS WESTWICK

During the early years of the Stanley Cup, sometimes people scratched their name into the Cup with a knife or nail file. Formal engraving did not begin until 1907. One of the most unusual names carved into the trophy was Thomas Westwick. He was the year-old son of Ottawa player Rat Westwick.

9. HAL WINKLER

The Boston Bruins won the Stanley Cup in 1929. Bruins goaltender Hal Winkler's name was inscribed on the Cup, even though he had been retired for a year.

10. 1988 EDMONTON OILERS

The Edmonton Oilers won the Stanley Cup in 1988. During the victory tour of Edmonton, the Cup was dented. It was repaired at an auto body shop.

Hockey Believe-It-or-Nots

H all of Fame goaltender Georges Vezina had 22 children. Ottawa goalie Fred Chittick refused to play in an 1898 Stanley Cup playoff game because he was not given enough complimentary tickets. Sometimes truth is stranger than fiction.

1. KEN DORATY

On April 3, 1933, the Toronto Maple Leafs and Boston Bruins played Game 5 of their Stanley Cup semifinal playoff series. After five overtimes, the game was still a scoreless tie. The exhausted teams agreed to decide the outcome by a coin toss. When the Toronto fans realized what was happening, they booed incessantly. The teams reluctantly decided to play on. In the sixth overtime, Toronto's Ken Doraty scored the winning goal as the Maple Leafs defeated the Bruins 1-0.

2. AL ROLLINS

Chicago Black Hawks goaltender Al Rollins had a 12-47-7 record during the 1953–1954 season. Despite the losing record, Rollins won the Hart Trophy as the NHL's Most Valuable Player. Voters decided that the Black

Hawks would have been even worse without Rollins in the net.

3. TOM MARTIN

In January 1983, the Seattle Breakers of the Western Hockey League (WHL) traded Tom Martin to Victoria. What made the trade unusual is that he was traded for a bus.

4. CY DENNENY

Ottawa's Cy Denneny led the NHL in scoring during the 1923–1924 season despite having only one assist. Denneny had 22 goals and one assist in 21 games. In those days the rules for being credited with an assist were less liberal than today.

5. BOBBY BAUN

On April 23, 1964, in the third period of Game 6 of the Stanley Cup finals between Toronto and Detroit, Maple Leafs defenseman Bobby Baun was struck in the leg by a slap shot. Baun was taken off the ice on a stretcher. In the dressing room, Baun's injured ankle was frozen to numb the pain and then taped. Incredibly, Baun insisted on returning to the game. Baun scored the game-winning goal in overtime as Toronto defeated Detroit 4 to 3 to even the series at three games apiece. An examination of Baun's injury revealed that he had scored the winning goal while playing on a broken ankle. Thanks to Baun's heroics, the Maple Leafs went on to win the Stanley Cup.

6. 1937–1938 CHICAGO BLACK HAWKS

The 1937–1938 Chicago Black Hawks finished the regular season with a record 14-25-9. The team barely qualified for the Stanley Cup playoffs, but no one expected them to go very far. The Black Hawks shocked the hockey world by winning the Stanley Cup.

7. TULSA OILERS

The Tulsa Oilers of the Central League had an unbelievable 1983–1984 season. Midway through the season, the Oilers experienced financial problems. The team suddenly had no owner and no home rink in which to play. Amazingly, the team decided to finish their season by playing the remainder of their schedule on the road. They practiced in shopping mall rinks and used tennis balls, out of the fear of damaging their hockey equipment. Incredibly, the Oilers won the league championship and were awarded the Jack Adams Award.

8. BABE SIEBERT

The 1929 game between the Montreal Maroons and the Boston Bruins was one of the most brutal on record. The Maroons spent the entire game hammering Boston's star player, Eddie Shore. Near the end of the game, Montreal's Babe Siebert high-sticked Shore. The Bruins' defenseman was unconscious for 15 minutes. He suffered a broken nose, four teeth knocked out, two black eyes, and several gashes on his face. Despite the flagrant foul, Babe Siebert was not even penalized.

9. LEN BURRAGE

In 1937, Len Burrage was the coach of the Manchester Rapids of the British Ice Hockey Association. Burrage also played defenseman for Harringay, a team in the same league. When the two teams played, the league

ordered Burrage to play for Harringay because he had
signed with them first.

10. MAURICE RICHARD

Maurice "the Rocket" Richard was one of the greatest
scorers in NHL history. Five times he led the NHL in
goals scored and he scored 541 goals during his career. Incredibly, Richard never led the NHL in scoring.
Although he was frequently among the league leaders
in goals scored, many players had more assists.

The One and Only

A l Secord of the Chicago Black Hawks was the only left winger to score four goals in a period. Detroit Red Wings Don Grosso was the only left winger to have six assists in an NHL game. Chicago Black Hawks Sam LoPresti was the only goaltender to make 80 saves in a game. The list features one-of-a-kind hockey feats.

1. KING CLANCY

The only player to play all six positions in a Stanley Cup game was King Clancy. The 20-year-old Ottawa Senators defenseman played goalie, both wings, center, and both defensive positions in the March 31, 1923, game against the Edmonton Eskimos. Ottawa won the game 1 to 0 to clinch the Stanley Cup title.

2. STAN MIKITA

Stan Mikita, right winger of the Chicago Black Hawks, is the only player to win the Ross Trophy, Hart Trophy, and Lady Byng Trophy in a season. Mikita was the Most Valuable Player, leading scorer, and was the most sportsmanlike player in the 1967 and 1968 seasons.

Frank Prazak/Hockey Hall of Fame

Stan Mikita is the only player to win the Ross Trophy,
Hart Trophy, and Lady Byng Trophy in one season.
Here he poses with the hardware in 1967 to prove it.

3. RON HEXTALL

The only NHL goaltender to score two goals was Philadelphia Flyers Ron Hextall. He scored a goal in a 5 to 2
victory over the Boston Bruins in a game played on
December 8, 1987. On April 11, 1989, Hextall scored
a second goal in an 8-5 win against the Washington
Capitals.

4. TERRY SAWCHUK

Goaltender Terry Sawchuk was the only player to be named rookie of the year in three different professional hockey leagues. Sawchuk was Rookie of the Year with the Omaha Knights of the United States Hockey League for the 1947–1948 season. The next year he was voted Rookie of the Year as a player for the Indianapolis Capitols of the American Hockey League. Sawchuk was the Calder Trophy winner with the National Hockey League's Detroit Red Wings in 1951.

5. PUNCH BROADBENT

Center Harry "Punch" Broadbent is the only player to score goals in 16 consecutive NHL games. Broadbent achieved the record as a member of the Ottawa Senators during the 1921–1922 season. He led the league in goals with 32 in 24 games.

6. AL MacINNIS

The only defenseman to lead the Stanley Cup playoffs in scoring was Al MacInnis of the Calgary Flames. MacInnis scored seven goals and had 24 assists to win the Smythe Trophy in 1989.

7. MATS NASLUND

Left winger Mats Naslund of the Montreal Canadiens is the only player to have five assists in an NHL All Star game. Naslund's performance led the Wales Conference to a 6 to 5 victory.

8. DALE HAWERCHUK

The only player to have five assists in one period was center Dale Hawerchuk of the Winnipeg Jets. Hawerchuk's five assists came in the second period of a 7-3 victory over the Los Angeles Kings on March 6, 1984.

9.   DUNC WILSON

Dunc Wilson of the Vancouver Canucks was the only goaltender in NHL history to allow three goals in a 20-second period. On February 25, 1971, Wilson was in the net in a game against the Boston Bruins. The score was tied 2-2 in the third period when John Bucyk, Ed Westfall, and Ted Green scored goals in a 20-second span. The Bruins won the game by the score of 8 to 3. Wilson had a 3-25-2 record for the season.

10.   JACK MARSHALL

The only player to be a member of four different Stanley Cup championship teams was Jack Marshall. He played on the 1901 Winnipeg Victories, 1902 Montreal AAA, 1907 and 1910 Montreal Wanderers, and the 1914 Toronto Blueshirts.

Hockey's Most Embarrassing Moments

When a hockey player makes a mistake, it usually proves costly. A few players have even scored goals for the other team. On the ice, there is no place to hide.

1. STEVE SMITH

Steve Smith has the dubious distinction of being the only player to hit the puck into his own goal in the deciding game of a Stanley Cup playoff series. On April 30, 1986, the Edmonton Oilers faced the Calgary Flames in the seventh game of the Stanley Cup division finals. With the score tied 2-2 in the third period, Edmonton defenseman Steve Smith tried to make a clearing pass. The errant pass struck the skate of the Oilers' goaltender Grant Fuhr and went into the net for the winning goal for Calgary. The goal was credited to center Perry Berezan, the closest Calgary player to the play.

2. ROB RAMAGE

On November 28, 1979, defenseman Rob Ramage of the Colorado Rockies scored a goal for the New York

Islanders. With the Rockies leading 4 to 3, Ramage sent a pass down the ice that went into his own net to tie the game. New York goaltender Billy Smith, the Islanders' player nearest Ramage, was credited with the goal. Luckily for Ramage, the Rockies rallied for a 7-4 win.

3. STEVE BUZINSKI

New York Rangers goaltender Steve Buzinski won only two games in his NHL career. Even when he made a good play, it seemed like it turned out disastrous. Buzinski caught a hard shot in his glove. As he attempted to pass it to the side of the net, Buzinski tossed the puck into his own net.

4. JOHN GARRETT

John Garrett tended goal for the Hartford Whalers from 1979 to 1982. In a game against Washington, Garrett was distracted by a Capital's goal that he believed did not cross the goal line. The perturbed goalie looked up at the scoreboard to watch a replay. While Garrett gazed at the screen, he did not notice that the referee had dropped the puck. Washington's All Star right winger Mike Gartner fired a shot past Garrett for a goal before he could react. Hartford coach Don Blackburn was so angry that he benched Garrett.

5. NOEL PICARD

St. Louis Blues defenseman Noel Picard wanted to hide his face after an embarrassing moment in a 1967 game against the Boston Bruins. Picard became disoriented and sat down on the Boston bench by mistake. The Bruins' players could barely help from laughing. On the other side of the rink, St. Louis coach Scotty Bowman was livid. Picard skated quickly across the ice and dove over the boards onto the Blues' bench. Unfortunately, the official saw him and penalized St. Louis for having too many players on the ice.

6. BOBBY HULL

Bobby Hull lost more than a fight in a WHA game. The Winnipeg Jets' star left winger got into an altercation with Birmingham Bulls defenseman Dave Hanson. In the middle of the fight, Hanson felt something soft in his hand. He had pulled off Hull's toupee. Freaked out, Hanson tossed the hairpiece across the ice.

7. EDDIE CONVEY

New York Americans forward Eddie Convey only scored one goal during his NHL career that lasted from 1931 to 1933. Convey couldn't even score when the other team tried to help. Convey was a friend of Toronto defenseman King Clancy. Clancy had heard that Convey might be sent to the minors if he did not produce soon. He convinced his goaltender Lorne Chabot to let Convey score a goal in a game in which they had a comfortable lead. Convey got the puck and Clancy let him go uncontested. Chabot left most of the net unguarded, but Convey somehow missed the net. They gave Convey a second chance and Convey's shot hit Chabot in the Adam's apple. As Chabot writhed on the ice, Clancy decided that Convey would have to score on his own.

8. DON CHERRY

One of the biggest blunders in Stanley Cup history occurred in Game 7 of the 1979 finals between the Boston Bruins and Montreal Canadiens. Boston led 4 to 3 with two and a half minutes remaining in the third period when Bruins coach Don Cherry sent one too many players on the ice. Boston was penalized and Montreal's Guy Lafleur scored the tying goal on the power play. Montreal left winger Yvon Lambert scored the game-winning goal in overtime. Bruins coach Don Cherry was fired.

9. HERB CAIN

Herb Cain was the NHL's leading scorer during the 1943–1944 season. The Montreal left winger had a moment he'd rather forget during a 1938 practice session. An area had been roped off behind the net of the practice rink for a drill. Cain did not see the rope and skated full speed toward the net. He was clotheslined and his feet flew into the air. Cain was knocked unconscious, but not seriously injured.

10. IAN TURNBULL

Ian Turnbull was a defenseman who played for the Toronto Maple Leafs from 1973 to 1981. During the 1980 season, Toronto Joe Crozier called a meeting to chastise the Maple Leafs' players for their lackadaisical play. Turnbull expressed his feelings about the meeting by letting out a loud fart.

Draft Bargains

Right winger Theoren Fleury, who was selected 166th in the 1987 NHL entry draft, became a 50-goal scorer for the Calgary Flames in 1991. Steve Larmer was the 120th pick of the 1980 draft and the Chicago Black Hawks' right winger scored 441 goals and more than 1,000 points during his career. Goaltender Ron Hextall, a winner of the Vezina and Smythe trophies in 1987, was the 119th selection of the 1982 NHL draft. None of these future stars were high draft choices.

1. DINO CICCARELLI

Right winger Dino Ciccarelli broke his leg as a junior skater. Wary of the injury, no NHL team drafted Ciccarelli. Signed as a free agent by the Minnesota North Stars, Ciccarelli proved the doubters wrong by scoring 608 goals in his NHL career.

2. DOMINIK HASEK

Czech goaltender Dominik Hasek was the 207th selection of the 1983 entry draft. Hasek was the 11th player selected that year by the Chicago Black Hawks. Hasek did not play in the NHL until the 1990–1991 season.

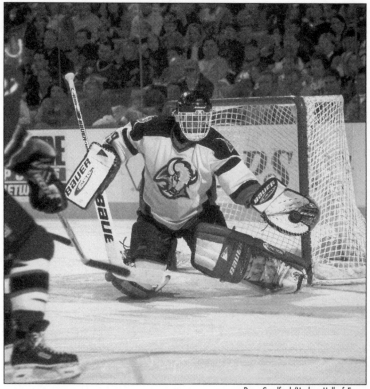

Dave Sandford/Hockey Hall of Fame

Taken late in the 1983 draft, Dominik Hasek has proven to
be quite the bargain, blossoming into one of today's
outstanding goaltenders and earning the nickname
"The Dominator" with saves like this one.

The Dominator became one of the best goalies in the
NHL and has won five Vezina trophies.

3. DAVE TAYLOR

Dave Taylor was the 210th selection of the 1975 amateur draft. Taylor was so little thought of that the Los
Angeles Kings selected 13 players ahead of him. The

right winger became a four-time All Star and scored 431 goals in his career.

4.   BRETT HULL

Despite being the son of hockey legend Bobby Hull, Brett Hull was the 117th selection of the 1984 draft. Hull exceeded all expectations by becoming one of the NHL's most prolific scorers. Three times he led the league in goals scored and only Wayne Gretzky has scored more than Hull's 86 goals during the 1990–1991 season.

5.   JARI KURRI

Right winger Jari Kurri was the 69th pick of the 1980 NHL entry draft. Kurri was a major reason the Edmonton Oilers dominated hockey in the late 1980s. The eight-time All Star scored 601 goals and 1,398 points in his NHL career.

6.   MARK MESSIER

Forty-seven players were selected before the Edmonton Oilers chose center Mark Messier. They never regretted their selection. Messier became a perennial All Star and one of the greatest scorers in NHL history.

7.   GLENN ANDERSON

Glenn Anderson was selected as the 69th overall pick of the 1979 entry draft by the Edmonton Oilers. The right winger was a four-time All Star and scored 498 goals and had 601 assists during his career.

8.   PATRICK ROY

The Montreal Canadiens selected goaltender Patrick Roy with the 51st pick in the 1984 NHL draft. The reason for Roy's low selection was his lack of success in the minor leagues. In his first season in the minors, Roy's record was 13-35-1. Roy became the first NHL goaltender to win 500 games.

9. ANDY MOOG

Goaltender Andy Moog was another draft bargain made by the Edmonton Oilers. He was selected 132nd in the 1980 NHL draft. Moog rewarded their confidence with a 143-53-21 record during his years in Edmonton.

10. PETE PEETERS

Pete Peeters was the 135th selection of the 1977 amateur draft. The goaltender had a 40-11-9 record with the Boston Bruins in 1983 and won the Vezina Trophy. A four-time All Star, Peeters had a 246-155-51 career record.

Draft Busts

Right winger Thomas Martin, the fifth pick in the 1964 amateur draft by the Toronto Maple Leafs, scored only one goal in the NHL. Defenseman Fred Arthur was the eighth overall pick of the 1980 draft by the Hartford Whalers. In 80 NHL games, Arthur scored one goal. Center Dan Gratton was the 10th selection of the 1985 draft, but he scored only one goal with the Los Angeles Kings. All of these highly touted prospects proved to be draft disappointments.

1. **CLAUDE GAUTHIER**

Claude Gauthier was the number one selection of the 1964 NHL entry draft by the Detroit Red Wings. Gauthier never played in the NHL.

2. **ANDRE VEILLEUX**

Right winger Andre Veilleux, the first pick of the 1965 NHL draft, was selected by the New York Rangers. Veilleux also never played in the NHL.

3. **RICK PAGNUTTI**

The Los Angeles Kings used the first pick of the 1967 draft to select Rick Pagnutti. The defenseman was another first-round selection who never played in an NHL game.

4.   TERRY CAFFERY

Center Terry Caffery was the third overall selection of the 1966 NHL draft. Selected by the Chicago Black Hawks, Caffery played in 14 NHL games and never scored a point.

5.   GARRY SWAIN

Pittsburgh selected center Gary Swain with the fourth pick of the 1968 NHL draft. Swain played in only nine NHL games and scored one goal.

6.   BJORN JOHANSSON

California's first pick in the 1976 draft was defenseman Bjorn Johansson. The Swede was the first player from outside of North America to be taken in the first round. Unfortunately, Johansson did not pan out and scored only one goal in his NHL career.

7.   SCOTT SCISSONS

The New York Islanders used their first pick of the 1990 draft to select Scott Scissons. The center was the sixth overall pick of the draft. Scissons played in only two NHL games and did not score.

8.   RON JONES

The Boston Bruins have had a history of great defensemen. Bobby Orr, Ray Bourque, and Eddie Shore all starred for the Bruins. Boston thought they had another gem when they drafted defenseman Ron Jones with the sixth pick of the 1971 draft. Jones was no Bobby Orr and scored one goal in 54 NHL games.

9.   GREG VAYDIK

Greg Vaydik was the seventh overall pick of the 1975 NHL draft by the Chicago Black Hawks. The center played in only five NHL games and did not score.

10.   ALEX STOJANOV

The Vancouver Canucks selected Alex Stojanov with the seventh overall pick of the 1991 NHL draft. The right winger scored 2 goals and had 5 assists in 107 games.

Minor League Wonders

Center Dave Gans scored more than 50 goals in OHL and IHL seasons, but never scored a goal in two brief stints in the NHL. Left winger Craig Endeen twice scored 50 goals in NHL seasons, but he never netted even one in the NHL. Stan Smrke scored 440 goals in the minor leagues, but the center did not score a goal in two seasons with the Montreal Canadiens. Many minor league sensations are unable to make it in the NHL.

1. GUYLE FIELDER

Guyle Fielder played professional hockey from 1947 to 1973. The center scored 600 goals and 10 times led his league in scoring. Fielder had two brief stints in the NHL. He played in three games with the Chicago Black Hawks during the 1950–1951 season and six games with the 1957–1958 Detroit Red Wings. Fielder never scored a point in the NHL.

2. DOUGLAS ADAM

Douglas Adam scored 519 goals during his professional hockey career. He led the Pacific Coast Hockey

League, WHL, and EHL in scoring. The left winger played in four games for the 1949–1950 New York Rangers, but he did not score a goal.

3. OSCAR HANSON

Oscar Hanson led various professional leagues in scoring five times. Hanson, a center, played in eight games with the Chicago Black Hawks in 1938 and did not score.

4. PAUL MESSIER

Paul Messier scored 425 goals during his professional hockey career. He was never confused with Mark Messier during his brief NHL career. In nine games with the 1978–1979 Colorado Rockies, the center was held scoreless.

5. EDDIE DOROHOY

Eddie Dorohoy was nicknamed the Great Gabbo. Four times the forward led leagues in assists. The forward played 16 games for the 1948–1949 Montreal Canadiens and was less than great. He did not score a point.

6. FRED BERRY

Fred Berry scored 452 goals during his professional career. Five times he scored more than 100 points in a season. The center played in three games with the Detroit Red Wings and did not score a point.

7. HARRY PIDHIRNY

Harry Pidhirny scored 469 goals in his professional hockey career that spanned 1944 to 1970. Pidhirny played two games at center for the 1957 Boston Bruins before being sent back to the minors.

8. KEVIN SCHAMEHORN

Right winger Kevin Schamehorn scored 433 goals as a professional. Between 1976 and 1981, Schamehorn had three brief stints with the Detroit Red Wings and Los Angeles Kings. He played in 10 NHL games and did not score a point.

9. JEANNOT GILBERT

Center Jeannot Gilbert had 442 career goals. Gilbert played in nine games for the Boston Bruins between 1962 and 1965 and scored one point.

10. BUCKY BUCHANAN

Bucky Buchanan scored 66 goals for the San Francisco Shamrocks of the PCHL in 1947. The forward player played 10 games in 1948 for the New York Rangers and did not score.

They Couldn't Win

E bbie Goodfellow had a 30-91-19 record as coach of the Chicago Black Hawks from 1950 to 1952. Lou Angotti, who coached the St. Louis Blues and Pittsburgh Penguins, had a career 22-78-12 record. Bill MacMillan, who had coaching stints in Colorado and New Jersey, won 41, lost 112, and had 27 ties. These coaches were among the least successful in NHL history.

1. EDDIE BUSH

Eddie Bush coached Kansas City for part of the 1975–1976 season. Bush's record as head coach was an abysmal 1-23-8.

2. JIM ANDERSON

Jim Anderson coached the Washington Capitals during the 1974–1975 season. The Capitals, under Anderson, had a 4-45-5 record.

3. LARRY WILSON

Larry Wilson coached the Detroit Red Wings for 36 games in the 1976–1977 season. The Red Wings had a 3-29-4 record with Wilson on the bench.

4.   COOPER SMEATON

The 1930–1931 Philadelphia Quakers were one of the worst teams in NHL history. Their coach was Cooper Smeaton. The Quakers had a terrible 4-36-3 record.

5.   FRED FREDRICKSON

Fred Fredrickson coached the 1929–1930 Pittsburgh Pirates to a 5-26-3 record. The team was so bad that the franchise folded.

6.   PHIL GOYETTE

Phil Goyette was a four-time All Star center with the Montreal Canadiens, New York Rangers, St. Louis Blues, and Buffalo Sabres. His ability as a player did not translate into coaching success. Goyette coached the 1972–1973 New York Islanders to a 6-38-4 record.

7.   TED LINDSAY

Ted Lindsay was an 11-time All Star as a player with the Detroit Red Wings and Chicago Black Hawks. Lindsay coached his old team, the Detroit Red Wings, for part of two seasons, and he had a 5-21-3 record.

8.   BRAD PARK

Brad Park was a Hall of Fame defenseman who played for the New York Rangers, Boston Bruins, and the Detroit Red Wings. Park was not destined to be a Hall of Fame coach. He coached the 1985–1986 Detroit Red Wings to a 9-34-2 record.

9.   GEORGE KINGSTON

George Kingston coached the San Jose Sharks from 1991 to 1993. His career coaching record was 28-129-

7. In his final season, the Sharks were 11-71-2, one of the worst seasons in NHL history.

10. PIT LEPINE

The Montreal Canadiens are the most successful franchise in NHL history. Pit Lepine coached the Canadiens during their worst season, 1939–1940. Montreal had a 15-game winless streak and a 10-33-5 record.

Colorful Coaches

Tom Webster, the Los Angeles Kings' coach from 1981 to 1992, once threw a hockey stick and hit a referee in the foot. Billy Reay, the coach of Buffalo of the American Hockey League, got into a fistfight with an announcer. Over the years, hockey has had its share of colorful coaches.

1. **FRED SHERO**

Fred Shero said of himself: "I don't live in the fast lane, I live in the off ramp." Shero coached the Philadelphia Flyers and New York Rangers between 1971 and 1981. During those years his teams had a record of 390-225-119. Shero was nicknamed the Fog because of an incident when he somehow managed to lock himself out of the Philadelphia arena. When he yelled to be let in, his voice sounded like a foghorn. Shero coached the championship teams in Philadelphia, which were nicknamed the Broad Street Bullies. The coach did not apologize for the team's rough play: "There's never been a death attributed to a hockey fight," Shero reasoned. "If you keep the opposition on their asses, they don't score goals," he said. Shero mused, "if the fans want to see pretty skating, let them go see a Sonja Henie movie." Shero befuddled his teams with seemingly pointless drills using tennis balls. Although some questioned his methods, no one questioned Shero's dedication to hockey. He summed up his attitude when he said, "Life is just a place where we spend between games."

2. DON CHERRY

Don Cherry was the head coach of the Boston Bruins from 1974 to 1979 and the Colorado Rockies from 1979 to 1980. His teams had a combined record of 250-153-77. The outspoken Cherry was nicknamed the Master of the Mouth. Cherry wore loud sports coats and said he consulted his bull terrier, Blue, on hockey decisions. He said Blue ignored him when the team lost. Cherry preferred old-fashioned hard-checking Canadian hockey and abhorred the European style that emphasized skating and passing. He inferred that some of the European players shied away from contact. After Soviet submarines entered Stockholm harbor Cherry cracked, "It was easy for the Commies to hide. They just put the subs in the corner. Everybody knows Swedes don't go into corners." When asked what he thought was the Europeans' contribution to hockey, Cherry replied, "The helmet, the visor, the dive." He said the Chicago Black Hawks were his favorite team because there weren't any European players on their roster. After Cherry wrote an autobiography he quipped, "Three years ago I couldn't spell author. Now I are one." Cherry once ordered one of his players to get rid of his tan because it made the rest of the players on the team look pale. When Cherry was fired as coach of the Colorado Rockies, a pundit said new coach Billy MacMillan would have "a big pair of lungs to fill."

3. HARRY NEALE

Harry Neale was coach of the Vancouver Canucks from 1978 to 1985 and the Detroit Red Wings from 1985 to 1986. Six of the seven years Neale coached, his teams had losing records. Neale joked, "We're losing at home, we can't win on the road. My failure as a coach is that I can't figure out any place else to play." He said, "I know my players don't like my practices, but that's OK because I don't like their games." The coach observed, "Our best system of forechecking is to shoot the puck in and leave it there." When Vancouver goaltender Curt Ridley injured both knees on a play, his coach said, "It's pretty good, but the NHL record is three." Asked when star winger Petr Klima was going to join the Red Wings, Neale answered, "The Czech is in the mail." Aware of the precarious nature of coaching, Neale said, "I sign a multi-minute contract."

4. GODFREY MATHESON

Godfrey Matheson coached the Chicago Black Hawks for two games during the 1932–1933 season. The coach devised a complex whistle system. One blow meant pass the puck. Two blows was a shot on goal. Three whistles was a defensive instruction, and so on. Players had trouble hearing the signals and were confused. They sometimes passed at the wrong time or took a shot when they shouldn't. Matheson was replaced after losing both of the games he coached.

5. BOB PULFORD

Bob Pulford coached the Los Angeles Kings and Chicago Black Hawks from 1972 to 1988. Pulford's NHL career record was 365-347-139. A man of few words, Pulford was nicknamed *Mute Rockne*. During the 1988 Stanley Cup playoffs against the St. Louis Blues, Pulford called for a strategy meeting with the Black Hawks' assistant coaches in an adjoining dressing room. When the coaches got locked into the room, a forklift was brought in to free them.

6. LESTER PATRICK

Lester Patrick coached the New York Rangers from 1926 to 1939. His teams had a 281-216-107 record. Patrick was known for his tightness with money. Rangers defenseman Babe Pratt said of Patrick: "He wouldn't give a worm to a blind bird." Patrick once instructed his team to drink a glass of hot water the first thing in the morning.

7. FRANK BOUCHER

Frank Boucher coached the New York Rangers from 1939 to 1949 and for the 1953–1954 season. Boucher endured some of the worst seasons in the Rangers' history. The 1943–1944 Rangers team won only 6 games and lost 39. Toward the end of his years with the Rangers, Boucher took his team to a hypnotist, David Tracy. The hypnotist tried to convince the Rangers' players that they were a winning team. The publicity stunt did not change the team's fortunes.

8. CHARLIE CONACHER

Charlie Conacher was coach of the Chicago Black Hawks from 1947 to 1950. Conacher was known for his temper both as a player and as a coach. After a 9-2 loss to the Detroit Red Wings, Conacher decked *Detroit*

Times writer Lew Walter. The sportswriter had written a negative column about the Black Hawks.

9.   EMILE FRANCIS

Emile Francis coached the New York Rangers from 1965 to 1975. The fiery Francis was not afraid to take on anyone. During a game against the Detroit Red Wings, Francis went into the crowd to fight with three fans in an argument about a disputed goal. His players had to come to his aid. Francis received a six-stitch cut on his face during the melee.

10.   MIKE KEENAN

Mike Keenan coached the New York Rangers to the 1994 Stanley Cup title. He also coached the Philadelphia Flyers and Chicago Black Hawks to the Stanley Cup finals. Keenan was nicknamed Captain Hook because he occasionally pulled his starting goalie to motivate his players. He was also known to throw pennies onto the ice to get a time-out.

Outrageous Owners

C ontroversial Edmonton Oilers owner Peter Pock-
lington inscribed his father's name on the Stanley
Cup and then was forced to have it x'd out. Bruce Norris, owner of the Detroit Red Wings, was criticized when
it was learned that the legendary Gordie Howe was only
the third highest paid player on the team. Meet some of
hockey's most outlandish owners.

1. EDDIE SHORE

When defenseman Eddie Shore retired as a player in
1940, he became owner of the Springfield Indians of
the American Hockey League. The rugged Shore had
more than his share of enemies as a player and was
even more disliked as an owner. He ordered his players
to be celibate until after the playoffs were over. He told
one of his players to comb his hair differently to im-
prove his skating. Shore made his players sell programs, paint seats, and even tap-dance in hotel
lobbies. Practices were held in darkened rinks. He tied
his goaltender to the net in an effort to make him stand
straighter. Shore tied another player's legs together because he thought the player skated with his legs too far

apart. The owner insisted on performing chiropractics on his unfortunate players, leaving them with more aches and pains than when he started. The eccentric Shore once traded a player for a hockey net. Known for his cheapness, Shore had incentives written into his players' contracts, then benched them when they came close to reaching them. Shore once locked a referee in the locker room because he thought he was biased against his team. Shore's reputation was so bad that some NHL players had it written into their contracts that they could not be sent down to Springfield. Shore did everything: parked cars, sold popcorn, and cleaned the arena. He operated the team until 1978.

2. **HAROLD BALLARD**

Harold Ballard became principal owner of the Toronto Maple Leafs in 1971. During the 1960s Ballard served a year in prison for tax evasion. Unrepentant, Ballard explained, "If you got a chance to screw the government out of a few bucks, you'd do it too." Ballard was so tight with his money that he drove 14 of his players to the rival World Hockey Association. When a streaker ran onto the ice during a game in Maple Leaf Gardens, Ballard said, "I was happy to have an attraction we didn't have to pay for." Ballard opposed having players' names on their uniforms because he feared it would hurt the program sales. He ordered that a large photo of Queen Elizabeth be torn down to add more seats. "She doesn't pay me anything. Besides, what position can she play?" Ballard asked. Ballard had some strange ideas. He got rid of players who were very religious: "I'm looking for guys you toss meat to and they'll go wild." On March 1, 1979, Ballard said he would fire coach Roger Neilson if the Maple Leafs lost to the Montreal Canadiens. When Toronto lost, the players vowed not to play if Neilson was fired. Ballard rehired Neilson but suggested he wear a bag over his head. The politically incorrect Ballard called a female CBC radio broadcaster a "dumb broad," and he once said, "Women are only good for lying on their backs." On Ballard's death, Wendell Clark commented, "I wish him luck wherever he goes."

3. FRED McLAUGHLIN

Major Frederic McLaughlin was commander of the Black Hawk regiment during World War I. When he founded an NHL hockey franchise in Chicago, he named them the Black Hawks. In 1937, McLaughlin announced he was going to have a team consisting entirely of American players. He even suggested he was going to change the team's name to the Chicago Yankees. The experiment quickly failed. McLaughlin frequently changed coaches. During one 9-year span, the Black Hawks had 11 different coaches. In 1932, McLaughlin met Godfrey Matheson on a train and hired him because he was impressed with his hockey knowledge. Matheson lasted two games as coach. Defenseman Taffy Abel led the Black Hawks to the Stanley Cup championship in 1934. When McLaughlin refused to give him a raise, Abel decided to retire. Another outrageous quirk: McLaughlin installed a straw man goalie to place in the net during shooting drills.

4. PERCY THOMPSON

Percy Thompson was the controversial owner of the Hamilton Tigers. His team had the best record in the NHL during the 1924–1925 season. The Tigers staged hockey's first strike. The players claimed that Thompson had promised to pay each of them a $200 bonus. When Thompson refused to pay the players, they went on strike. NHL president Frank Calder suspended the players and fined them each $200. Thompson lost not only the chance to win the Stanley Cup, but the Hamilton franchise as well. Thompson sold his team to the New York Americans for $75,000.

5. SAM LICHTENHEIN

Sam Lichtenhein was the owner of the Montreal Wanderers. Known for his frugality, Lichtenhein set a pay ceiling of $600 in 1914. Unhappy with his team's performance, in February 1915 he issued an ultimatum; shape up or play without pay for the rest of the season. Lichtenhein hired private investigators to keep his players under surveillance. The Montreal Wanderers were one of the original NHL teams in 1917. A few games into the season, a fire burned the Montreal Arena to the ground. Lichtenhein attempted to borrow players from other teams to continue. Unsuccessful in his attempt to find players and a new arena, Lichtenhein allowed the Wanderers' franchise to fold.

6. LEO DANDURAND

Leo Dandurand bought the Montreal Canadiens in 1921 for $11,000. Dandurand coached the Canadiens for three seasons: 1921, 1925, and 1934. He prohibited his players from driving automobiles because he believed it caused cramps in their hands and legs. Dandurand also founded the Montreal Alouettes football team. When Dandurand decided to sell the team in 1935, he considered selling it to investors who wanted to move the Canadiens to Cleveland. Fortunately for

Montreal, Dandurand sold the team to investors who kept the team in the Canadian city.

7. WILLIAM DWYER

The owner of the New York Americans of the National Hockey League from 1925 to 1941, William Dwyer was a convicted bootlegger. While owner, Big Bill spent 13 months in Atlanta Federal Penitentiary.

8. CONN SMYTHE

The legendary Conn Smythe purchased the Toronto St. Patricks in 1927 and renamed them the Maple Leafs. Smythe helped turn the Maple Leafs into a perennial NHL power. In 1930, Smythe wanted to purchase the contract of Ottawa defenseman King Clancy, but he did not have the $35,000 asking price. He entered Rare Jewel, a filly he bought for $250 in a stakes race at Toronto's Woodbine Race Track. Smythe bet on the 107-1 long shot and won $15,570. He used the winnings to acquire Clancy. Smythe was never afraid to antagonize opposing players and fans. He took out an ad in a Boston newspaper urging the fans to come out and see the Maple Leafs perform hockey the way it should be played. Smythe once punched a Boston fan during a melee in December 1933. While trying to get at an official, Smythe struck New York Rangers player Art Coulter. In a game against the Montreal Canadiens, Smythe placed an usher's hat on referee Mike Rodden.

9. CHARLES O. FINLEY

Charles O. Finley is best remembered for being the owner of baseball's Oakland A's, the World Series champions in 1972, 1973, and 1974. In 1970, Finley bought the Oakland Seals of the NHL. As with the Oakland A's, Finley changed the color of the Seals' jerseys to green and yellow. Their white skates made them look like figure skaters. The Seals could never match the success of the A's and Finley sold the team in February 1974.

10.   BENNY LEONARD

Benny Leonard won the lightweight boxing title in 1917 and was elected to the Boxing Hall of Fame in 1955. Leonard was the owner of the Philadelphia Quakers of the NHL for the 1930–1931 season. After a 4-36-4 record, one of the worst in NHL history, the Quakers disbanded.

Ice Flakes

L eft wing Eddie "the Entertainer" Shack skated with such abandon that Punch Imlach said that he could play all three forward positions at the same time. Laurie Scott, a forward who played for the New York Rangers in the late 1920s, was one of the most superstitious hockey players. He never shaved before a game and insisted on being the last player to leave the dressing room. He always set his stick blades in the same direction in front of his locker. When teammate Leo Reise turned them the other way, Scott threatened to retire from hockey. Defenseman Barclay Plager said, "You don't have to be crazy to play hockey, but it helps." All of these players exhibited behavior that was out of the ordinary.

1. KING CLANCY

Twenty-year-old defenseman King Clancy was a member of the 1923 Ottawa Senators, Stanley Cup champions. He took the Cup home to show his father. The next year no one could locate the Cup until Clancy remembered it was still sitting on his mantel. Conn Smythe said of Clancy: "He scored hockey by the number of fights. If you lost 7 to 1, but won five fights, he figured you won the game." Clancy once challenged a heckling fan in Boston to a fight only to discover he was Heavyweight Boxing Champion Jack Sharkey. On another occasion, Clancy struck Eddie Shore while kneeling on the ice. The fearsome Shore challenged him to do it again. Clancy said he would only if Shore would get back on his hands and knees. During a game in Toronto, a doctor was mercilessly heckling him. Clancy replied, "Maybe I'm not perfect, Doc, but I don't bury my mistakes like you do."

2.   GUMP WORSLEY

Goaltender Gump Worsley commented that 90 percent of goalies were crazy. While playing for the hapless New York Rangers teams of the early 1950s, Worsley was asked what team gave him the most trouble. Gump did not hesitate to answer, "The Rangers." Worsley said of goaltending: "The only job worse is a javelin catcher at a track and field meet." Worsley hated practice. "I get enough practice during the game," he reasoned. Gump refused to wear a mask. "My face is my mask," he said. "Would it be fair not to give the fans the chance to see my beautiful face?"

3.   GILLES GRATTON

Gilles Gratton played in the NHL from 1975 to 1977. Enforcer John Ferguson called the goaltender "Gratoony the Loony." Gratton believed in reincarnation. He claimed that in a former life he was an officer during the Franco–Prussian War. The soldier suffered a leg wound and Gratton said the injury bothered him during games. During another reincarnation, Gratton said he was run through by a lance during the Spanish Inquisition. He attributed his stomach problems to the wound. Gratton believed he had stoned people in biblical times and he was being repaid by having pucks shot at his head. Occasionally, Gratton streaked during practice.

4. MIKE WALTON

Center Mike "Shaky" Walton played in the NHL from 1965 to 1979. When Toronto Maple Leafs coach Punch Imlach banned long hair on the team, Walton protested by wearing a Beatles wig. While playing for the Minnesota Fighting Saints of the WHA, he wore his uniform to a bar after a game. On another occasion, he dove into a pool while wearing full hockey gear. Walton did a television interview wearing only shaving cream covering his private parts.

5. NICK FOTIU

Nick Fotiu played left winger for the New York Rangers, Hartford Whalers, Calgary Flames, Philadelphia Flyers, and Edmonton Oilers. Fotiu was one of hockey's top practical jokers. He enjoyed putting black shoe polish on telephone receivers and whipped cream on restaurant trays. Fotiu placed a live lobster on the chest of sleeping Bill Goldsworthy, nearly scaring his roommate to death. Aware of Phil Esposito's fear of insects, he hid cockroaches in his uniform. Fotiu filled goaltender John Davidson's car with garbage.

6. GUY LAPOINTE

Another shameless practical joker was Guy Lapointe. The Hall of Fame defenseman cut holes in the hats of his Montreal teammates and nailed their shoes to the floor. He knew Phil Esposito would not take a shower without wearing his sandals, so Lapointe taped them to the dressing room floor.

7. **DEREK SANDERSON**

Derek Sanderson played center for the Boston Bruins from 1966 to 1974. A hockey heartthrob, Sanderson rated NHL cities by how attractive the women were. He rated Los Angeles among the best cities, and Pittsburgh the worst. Boston radio station WBZ ran an essay contest in which women could explain in 103 words or less why they wanted a lunch date with Sanderson. More than 13,000 entries were received and the winner was a 73-year-old woman with 12 grandchildren. The sharp dressing ladies' man was a partner with New York Jets quarterback Joe Namath in the Boston night spot, Bachelors III. Derek was not the only flaky family member. Sanderson's father kept his son's stitches in a jar.

8. **BRENDAN SHANAHAN**

Left winger Brendan Shanahan scored more than 50 goals during the 1993 and 1994 seasons with the St. Louis Blues. Although he has had many accomplishments during his hockey career, Shanahan liked to embellish his résumé in the media guide. Shanahan's biography said that he made his film debut in *Forrest Gump*. Other false claims were that he was a ballboy at the 1994 U.S. Open Tennis Championships and that he was a goalkeeper for Ireland at the 1994 World Cup soccer tournament.

9. **DIDIER PITRE**

Didier Pitre was one of the flashiest players of the early days of hockey. He was the first player to spit up shreds

of ice with his quick stops. Between periods, Pitre
drank a pint of champagne.

10. CHARLIE CONACHER

Charlie Conacher once held roommate Baldy Cotton
out of a seventh-floor window to settle an argument.
Conacher also tied and gagged King Clancy to a chair
in his hotel room.

Money Matters

A t the turn of the twentieth century, star hockey players earned around $30 a week and most had to work a second job to make a living. Joe Malone led the league in scoring in the NHL's first season with 44 goals in 20 games. His salary for the exceptional season was $1,000. Hockey has not always been a big-money sport.

1. BILLY NICHOLSON

A century ago, Haileybury defeated Cobalt in overtime in a hockey game played in Northern Ontario. There was a large amount of betting in the game. When Haileybury scored the winning goal, appreciative fans threw money onto the ice. Players scrambled to get their share. Billy Nicholson, Haileybury's 300-pound goaltender, grabbed a washtub to collect the cash. When he was done, he turned the washtub upside down and sat on it to protect his stash of cash.

2. CHARLES DINSMORE

Center Charles Dinsmore played center for the Montreal Maroons from 1924 to 1927. In 1930, Dinsmore attempted to make a comeback. He was so determined to play that he accepted a salary of a dollar a year. After being held scoreless in nine games, Montreal decided Dinsmore was not worth a buck and released him.

3. JACK GIBSON

In 1902, star amateur hockey player Jack Gibson accepted a silver dollar from the townspeople of Berlin, Ontario, as a token of their appreciation after he led their team to the league championship. Because he accepted money, Gibson was stripped of his amateur status. Unable to play amateur hockey, Gibson opened a dental practice. In 1905, Gibson organized the first professional hockey league.

4. KEN RANDALL

Ken Randall of the Toronto Arenas was suspended for a week in February 1918 for arguing with officials. The NHL offered to shorten the suspension if Randall agreed to pay a $15 fine and $20 in overdue fines. Randall was able to scrape together $32 in cash and three dollars' worth of pennies. When the NHL refused to accept the pennies, Randall filled a bag with pennies and threw it onto the ice during a game with Ottawa. An Ottawa player tore open the bag with his stick and spread the pennies all over the ice. The game was stopped while players picked up all the pennies.

5. BILL EZINICKI

"Wild Bill" Ezinicki was a rugged right winger with the Toronto Maple Leafs in the 1940s. Ezinicki had an insurance contract in which he was paid $5 for every stitch he received. In one encounter with Detroit's Terrible Ted Lindsay, he collected $100 for a 20-stitch cut. Unfortunately, he lost money when he was fined $300 by the NHL for rough play.

6.   BUCKO McDONALD

On March 24, 1936, the Detroit Red Wings played a six overtime playoff game against the Montreal Maroons. A Detroit fan offered Red Wings defenseman Bucko McDonald $5 for every Montreal player he knocked down. McDonald sent 37 Maroon players sprawling and collected $185.

7.   HARRY JACOBSON

On April 4, 1942, the Detroit Red Wings defeated the Toronto Maple Leafs 3-2 in Game 1 of the Stanley Cup finals. After the game, Harry Jacobson, who considered himself to be the Red Wings' number one fan, distributed $115 he had raised to the Detroit players. The Red Wings won the first three games, then lost four in a row to lose the Stanley Cup to the Maple Leafs.

8.   CONN SMYTHE

Today, the television rights to hockey games cost networks millions of dollars per season. In the first year of the famed hockey broadcast, *Hockey Night in Canada*, Conn Smythe of the Toronto Maple Leafs charged $100 for the team's television rights.

9.   FRANK CALDER

Frank Calder was the first president of the National Hockey League. During his first season as president, Calder was paid $800.

10. KING CLANCY

Hall of Fame defenseman King Clancy signed a three-year contract with the Ottawa Senators in 1921. Clancy's salary was $400 per year with a $100 signing bonus.

Memorable Memorabilia

S tar goaltender Patrick Roy owns a valuable collection of hockey memorabilia. Among his most treasured items is a rare set of 1912 hockey cards. From autographs to hockey cards, hockey memorabilia is extremely collectible.

1. PAUL CAVALLINI

In a game played on December 22, 1990, St. Louis Blues defenseman Paul Cavallini lost a tip of a finger when he was struck with a slap shot off the stick of Chicago's Doug Wilson. The fingertip was stolen by a clerk in the pathology department. Cavallini was horrified to learn that a St. Louis radio station created a promotion to auction the severed fingertip. "It was sick," Cavallini said.

2. HOCKEY FIGHTS CANCER

Hockey Fights Cancer is an annual charity event that has raised more than $4 million for cancer research. Celebrities paint designs on hockey masks, which are auctioned to raise money to fight the deadly disease. Celebrities who have painted masks include Mel Gibson,

Gene Hackman, Rob Lowe, Martin Sheen, Michael J. Fox, Jay Leno, Pierce Brosnan, Ricky Martin, and Britney Spears.

3. GEORGES VEZINA

In the Game, a company that makes hockey cards, found a way for its customers to own a piece of hockey history. The company cut up valuable items of hockey memorabilia so it could place them in selected packs of hockey cards. An 80-year-old pair of gloves used by legendary goaltender Georges Vezina was one of the items cut into little pieces. The gloves were valued at $25,000. Other items cut to pieces included Terry Sawchuk's blocker, the stick of Johnny Bower, gloves used by Jacques Plante and Turk Broda, and Vladislav Tretiak's jersey. Many hockey purists protested the destruction of the rare pieces of hockey equipment.

4. BOBBY HULL

Beehive Corn Syrup used to offer a deal in which collectors could send in labels in exchange for hockey cards. Bobby Hull recalled that as a child he rummaged through neighbors' garbage cans to find the prized labels.

5. 1974 PHILADELPHIA FLYERS

In 1974, the city of Philadelphia held a parade to honor the Stanley Cup champions, the Philadelphia Flyers. The players waved to the crowd while seated in convertibles. A few of the players drank too much in the celebration and had to stop to go to the bathroom. Many fans were startled to see their heroes standing at their door. In exchange for letting them use their bathrooms, Flyers players signed autographs.

6. MAURICE RICHARD

During the 1952–1953 season, Maurice Richard of the Montreal Canadiens scored his 325th goal to pass Nels Stewart as the NHL's all-time leading goal scorer. The puck was plated with gold and presented to England's Queen Elizabeth.

7. BERT CORBEAU

Bert "Old Pig Iron" Corbeau was a defenseman who played in the NHL from 1917 to 1927. Although he was not among hockey's greatest players, one of his hockey cards is the most valuable. A rare 1923 V 145-1 card is valued at more than $20,000. Only 10 of the cards are known to exist.

8. SPRAGUE CLEGHORN

A 1924 card of defenseman Sprague Cleghorn is valued at more than $10,000. The card, part of the Maple Crispette set, is rare, because few were produced in order to make the set more difficult to complete.

9. FRANK MAHOVLICH

The 1968 Topps card of star left winger Frank Mahovlich is highly collectible because it's an oddity. Mahovlich's head was placed on another player's body.

10. PHIL ESPOSITO

When Phil Esposito posed for his 1971 Topps card, Esposito wore his Boston Bruins jersey over his street clothes. His pants are clearly visible in the photo.

Hockey Fanatics

Sixty-five-year-old Toronto Maple Leafs George Crawford elbowed Flyers goon Dave Schultz in the face. A female New York Rangers fan stuck Toronto's Bill Ezinicki with a hatpin during a game. In 1972, a Vancouver fan pulled the hair of Flyers intimidator Don Saleski, who was choking Canucks defenseman Barry Wilkins. In an 1898 game in Ottawa, Weldon Young went into the stands to confront some hecklers and was beaten to a bloody pulp. At the Los Angeles Forum, three voluptuous women streaked during a Kings game. Ned Harkness had a 12-22-4 record during a brief stint as coach of the Detroit Red Wings during the 1970–1971 season. Harkness was so unpopular that Detroit fans broke his car windows, egged his house, and sent him death threats. One fan even attacked him. On Mug Night, angry New York Rangers fans hurled plastic mugs onto the ice, prompting one player to remark, "I'm just glad it wasn't Machete Night."

1. MAURICE RICHARD

Montreal's Maurice Richard was suspended for the remainder of the 1955 season by NHL president Clarence

Campbell for striking linesman Cliff Thompson during a game against the Boston Bruins. The suspension cost Richard a chance to win the league scoring title. As a result, Montreal fans were in an ugly mood on March 17, 1955, when the Canadiens played the Detroit Red Wings at the Forum. Clarence Campbell was pelted with fruit, eggs, rotten vegetables, pickled pigs' feet, and bottles. One fan offered to shake Campbell's hand, then slugged the league president. Another fan crushed two ripe tomatoes on Campbell's chest. Fans threw garbage onto the ice and once tossed a tear gas bomb. The Red Wings were leading 4-1 when fans began to riot. They threw bricks through hundreds of windows at the Forum. A mob of more than 10,000 people roamed the streets of Montreal, smashing windows of automobiles and throwing rocks at police. Stores were looted, fires set, and automobiles overturned. Seventy people were arrested and damage was estimated at more than $500,000.

2. ROY SPENCER

Roy Spencer was the father of Toronto Maple Leafs left winger Brian Spencer. On December 12, 1970, Spencer hoped to see his son, a rookie, play on television in a game against the Buffalo Sabres. He was outraged when he discovered that the Vancouver–California game was being telecast instead of the Toronto game. Spencer drove 70 miles to the CBC affiliate in Prince George. At gunpoint, he ordered the station to switch to the Maple Leafs game. In a confrontation with police, Roy Spencer was shot to death.

3.   1985 QUEBEC FANS

On February 23, 1895, Quebec lost to Ottawa by the score of 3 to 2. Ottawa fans were upset because two Quebec players, Archie Scott and David Watson, were expelled for rough play. The fans were further angered when a Quebec goal that would have tied the game was disallowed. A mob of Quebec supporters followed the officials to the train station. They dragged umpire Jack Findlay and a referee named Hamilton back to the arena. The fans twisted the officials' arms, demanding that the game be declared a tie. Police were called in to save the men from further harm. Quebec was suspended for the rest of the season to ensure the officials' safety.

4.   1917 QUEBEC FANS

Twenty-two years after the Quebec fans attacked the officials in a game against Ottawa, they again rioted in a game versus the Toronto Blueshirts. On February 3, 1917, Quebec led Toronto 7 to 3 late in the game when the fans lost control. The game had been extremely roughly played and several players had been hurt. Toronto's Ken Randall was hit in the mouth by a fan. Randall climbed into the stands and beat up the fan who assaulted him. The fans rioted and began hitting the Toronto players with chairs and bottles. Some fans chased the players to the train station, where the players were assaulted again.

5.   1937 LONDON FANS

The 1937 World Amateur Hockey Championship was held in London, England, at the Harringay Arena. A team from Canada called the Kimberly B.C. Dynamiters defeated the team from Great Britain 3 to 0. British fans, displeased with the result, chased the Belgian official named Poplemont from the arena. They showered the ice with fruit, garbage, and beer bottles. The fans then turned on the Canadian players, who fought for their lives. An ingenious bandleader began playing "God Save the Queen." The English fans immediately stopped rioting and stood at attention. When the music stopped, they quietly left the arena.

6. MILLIONAIRE'S ROW

Ottawa fans were not known for their hospitality to opposing players during the 1910s. During a game against the Montreal Wanderers, Ottawa goaltender Percy LeSueur left the ice and sat down in a section of the stands known as Millionaire's Row. LeSueur encouraged the fans to pelt Montreal goalie Billy Nicholson with rotten eggs, cigars, programs, and anything else they could lay their hands on.

7. ERIC STEINER

During the 1959–1960 season, the New York Rangers and Detroit Red Wings played to a 2-2 tie. As he left the ice, New York center Camille "the Eel" Henry had his stick taken by a fan named Eric Steiner. When Henry tried to grab the stick, the fan hit him in the face. Henry, still wearing his hockey skates, chased Steiner out of the arena and down the street. Finally, Henry tackled the fan and regained his stick.

8. AUREL JOLIAT

Montreal Canadiens left winger Aurel Joliat had a well-known feud with Hooley Smith of the Montreal Maroons. One night Joliat was chasing Smith along the boards when the local chief of police reached out and grabbed Joliat. He dragged the policeman onto the ice and tore off his coonskin coat. Joliat claimed it was the only fight he ever won on the ice.

9.   1972 PHILADELPHIA BLAZERS' FANS

In 1972 the Philadelphia Blazers of the World Hockey Association played their first home game against the New England Whalers. Fans were given souvenir pucks to commemorate the occasion. The Zamboni machines did not work properly, leaving the ice choppy and cracking. The game had to be postponed. Blazers player Derek Sanderson was given the unenviable task of telling the fans the game was being postponed. Irate fans hurled hundreds of pucks onto the ice.

10.   SCOTT MELLANBY

Prior to a game against the Calgary Flames, Scott Mellanby, a right winger for the Florida Panthers, killed a rat in the dressing room. That night he scored two goals in a 4-3 Florida victory. Panthers fans referred to the feat as a rat trick. During the 1995–1996 season, they threw plastic rats onto the ice when Mellanby scored.

Official Business

Games of the NHL were officiated by local referees until 1926 when full-time officials were hired. Odie Cleghorn, one of the most penalized players of his day, became an official after he retired. Referee Hugh Nelson was attacked by Montreal's Maurice Richard in New York's Picadilly Hotel because he failed to call a penalty when the Rocket was tripped in a game against Boston the previous night. Since hockey's beginnings, officials have been the center of controversy.

1. JIM FINDLAY

The 1899 Stanley Cup finals was a best-of-three series between Montreal and Winnipeg. Montreal won the first game and led 3-2 in Game 2, when Winnipeg's Tony Gingras was slashed on his leg by Montreal's Bob Mc-Dougall. When referee Jim Findlay called a two-minute penalty, the Winnipeg players complained that it was not enough. The Winnipeg players left the ice in protest. Findlay, offended that his officiating was criticized, also left the rink. Montreal players chased him in a sleigh and convinced him to return. Findlay forfeited the game and the Stanley Cup to Montreal.

2. GARRY HOWATT AND MICKEY VOLCAN

On January 15, 1983, a blizzard prevented referee Ron Fournier and linesman Dan Marovelli from arriving in time for a game between the New York Islanders and Hartford Whalers. Linesman Ron Foyt appointed New York left winger Garry Howatt and Hartford defenseman Mickey Volcan as officials. The players served as officials in the first period until the real officials arrived.

3. CLARENCE CAMPBELL

Clarence Campbell was president of the National Hockey League from 1946 to 1971. Earlier in his career, Campbell was an NHL referee. During a 1937 playoff game, Dit Clapper of the Boston Bruins and Dave Trottier of the Montreal Maroons got into a fight. Clapper was giving Trottier a beating when Campbell tried to pull him off by his hair. Clapper turned around and decked Campbell and Clapper was fined $100 for punching the future NHL president.

4. BILL STEWART

The Chicago Black Hawks and Boston Bruins played a game on March 14, 1933, that ended in a wild melee. Chicago coach Tommy Gorman was livid when referee Bill Stewart allowed a disputed goal by Boston. Gorman yanked Stewart's sweater over his head and the two men exchanged blows. The police pulled Gorman off Stewart and the game was forfeited to Boston. Ironically, Stewart later became a coach and led the Chicago Black Hawks to the Stanley Cup title in 1938.

5. COOPER SMEATON

Cooper Smeaton was a Hall of Fame referee who had his share of controversy. On January 16, 1921, Smeaton refereed a game between the Ottawa Senators and the Montreal Canadiens. With five minutes left in the game, the Ottawa players left the ice in protest of Smeaton's calls. Newsy Lalonde and Amos Arbour scored uncontested goals in a 5 to 3 Montreal victory.

6. GEORGE HAYES

Despite being fired for bad eyesight, linesman George Hayes was elected to the Hockey Hall of Fame in 1988. Hayes once threatened to throw the referee-in-chief off a moving train. He got into a fight in a restaurant and could not see for two weeks after he was hit over the head with a ketchup bottle. Hayes was fired in 1965 when he refused to take an eye test. He insisted that he had tested his eyes by reading the labels off liquor bottles in a Montreal bar.

7. RED STOREY

Red Storey was another Hall of Fame official whose career ended in controversy. On April 4, 1959, Storey refereed Game 6 of the Stanley Cup semifinal series between the Montreal Canadiens and the Chicago Black Hawks. Montreal won the game 5 to 4. Chicago coach Rudy Pilous charged that Storey had not called two late penalties against the Canadiens. A Montreal fan doused Storey with beer and another jumped on his back. The next day NHL president Clarence Campbell said that Storey had "froze." Storey, stung by the criticism, resigned.

8. CHING JOHNSON

Ching Johnson was a hard-hitting defenseman who played in the NHL from 1926 to 1938. After he retired as a player, Johnson was a minor league referee. Fans

were shocked when the referee inexplicably body-
checked a player. "The old habit was too deep within
me," Johnson admitted, "I forgot where I was and what
I was doing."

9. GEORGE GRAVEL

George "Gertie" Gravel was a colorful official in the
1940s. A fan once threw a fish at him. When Detroit's
Ted Lindsay took a dive to try to draw a penalty, Gravel
leaned over the fallen Red Wing and said, "The ice is
too hard for diving and you can't swim in it either."

10. DALTON McARTHUR

Referee Dalton McArthur was struck by Montreal Canadiens coach Toe Blake during Game 3 of the 1961
Stanley Cup semifinal series against the Chicago Black
Hawks. Blake was fined $2,000 as a result of the inci-
dent.

The Extra Edge

Center Tom Lysiak said, "Everyone cheats in hockey." Deception has been used for a variety of reasons in hockey.

1. TOM LOCKHART

Tom Lockhart has been called "The Bill Veeck of Hockey." Lockhart was known for his outrageous promotional ideas. In his first year as president of the Eastern Hockey League, Lockhart made up phony games to fill out the schedule. He sent the scores of 21 games that were never played to the newspapers.

2. JOHNNY OOGLENOOK

Chicago Black Hawks publicity director Joe Farrell had some fun with a cub reporter. In the early 1940s, Farrell told a young reporter that he had signed an Eskimo player named Johnny Ooglenook, whose name meant "Great Whale Hunter." Farrell raved that Ooglenook was a terrific skater and a brilliant stickhandler. The gullible reporter believed him, but Farrell let him in on the joke before he published the story.

3. RAINEY DRINKWATER

In 1926, the New York Americans signed a Canadian named Rene Boileau. In a publicity stunt, the team said Boileau's name was Rainey Drinkwater and he was an Indian from the Cauhnawaga Indian Reservation. Boileau played in only seven games and did not score.

4. TARO TSUJIMOTO

In the 12th round of the 1974 NHL entry draft, the Buffalo Sabres selected Taro Tsujimoto. The Sabres said that the unknown player was a center who played in Tokyo. Tsujimoto was the first Asian to be drafted by an NHL team. Buffalo general manager Punch Imlach later admitted that it was all a hoax. There was no hockey player named Taro Tsujimoto. Imlach had found the name in the Buffalo phone book.

5. RAY BOURQUE

The great Boston Bruins defenseman Ray Bourque was accused by the Montreal Canadiens of biting a blood capsule to draw a penalty. Bourque denied the accusation. "Do they think this is the World Wrestling Federation?" he asked.

6. WELDON YOUNG

Ottawa's Weldon Young was notorious for his "fainting" to draw a penalty. In an 1895 game against Quebec, Young made one of his famous dives. Quebec's Dolly Swift was not amused. He doused Young with a bucket of water to "revive" him.

7. OTTAWA SILVER SEVEN

The Rat Portage Thistles defeated the favored Ottawa Silver Seven 9 to 3 in Game 1 of their 1905 Stanley Cup challenge. The Thistles were using new tube skates that allowed them to skate faster. Prior to Game 2, Ottawa flooded the rink and used salt to soften the ice in order to slow the Rat Portage skaters. The play worked and Ottawa won Games 2 and 3 to win the Cup.

8. BRANTFORD FANS

In the early days of hockey, fans sometimes attempted to influence the outcome of a game. Brantford fans offered referee Jimmy Fraser $10 if he ensured that their team won a game against Preston. Fraser refused the bribe and Preston won on a last-second goal. After the game the Brantford fans offered Fraser $15 if he would declare that the goal had come after time expired. Fraser once again refused.

9. CONN SMYTHE

During the 1936–1937 season, Toronto Maple Leafs owner Conn Smythe accused the Montreal Maroons of blunting the skates of his players by spreading sand on the floor of the locker room. The charges were never substantiated.

10. CLINT BENEDICT

In the early years of the NHL, it was illegal for a goaltender to go to his knees to make a save. Ottawa Senators goalie Clint Benedict was a master of "flopping," a technique of pretending to lose his balance. Fans yelled, "Get a mattress." Players who were caught flopping were fined $2 until 1918, when it was legalized.

Goons

Toronto defenseman Red Horner led the NHL in penalty minutes for eight consecutive years from 1932 to 1940. On March 11, 1979, Randy Holt was assessed a record 67 minutes in penalties in a game against the Philadelphia Flyers, an impressive feat considering the game lasted 60 minutes. Boston's Chris Nolan set a dubious record by being whistled for 10 penalties in a game against Hartford played on March 31, 1991. Defenseman Steve "Demolition Derby" Durbano was assessed 1,127 penalty minutes in 220 NHL games. Most hockey teams have tough guys to protect their star players and intimidate opposing players. Whether you call them goons or enforcers, they are hockey's most feared players.

1. TIGER WILLIAMS

Dave "Tiger" Williams terrorized NHL opponents from 1974 to 1988. The left winger was assessed a record 3,966 penalty minutes in his career. Williams said, "I want people to remember Tiger Williams as more than just a punch in the mouth." Pittsburgh Penguins defenseman Dennis Owchar remembered Williams for the 46-stitch gash he suffered when he hit him with a stick in a 1976 game. Williams hit Buffalo's coach Scotty Bowman with his stick on the Sabres' bench. Tiger bit Dave Schultz so hard that he left his teeth marks on his skin. In 1982, Williams was suspended for seven games for hitting New York Islanders goaltender Billy Smith in the head with his stick and attempting to choke him.

2. DAVE SCHULTZ

If anyone could challenge Tiger Williams as hockey's premier goon, it was left winger Dave "the Hammer" Schultz. He summed up his philosophy when he said, "Hockey is a contact sport. It's not the Ice Follies." The biggest bully of the Philadelphia Flyers' notorious Broad Street Bullies, Schultz set a Stanley Cup playoff record when he was penalized 42 minutes in a game against Toronto on April 22, 1976. In the 1974–1975 season, Schultz set an NHL record with 472 penalty minutes.

3. BILLY COUTU

Billy "Beaver" Coutu was one of the NHL's first goons. The defenseman played for Montreal, Hamilton, and Boston between 1917 and 1927. In 1923, Montreal Canadiens owner Leo Dandurand was so appalled by Coutu's violent play that he suspended him. Coutu was suspended from the NHL for life in 1927 after attacking officials Billy Bell and Gerry LaFlamme in a game against Ottawa.

4. CULLY WILSON

Another early ruffian was right winger Cully Wilson, who played in the NHL from 1919 to 1927. In 1919,

London Life-Portnoy/Hockey Hall of Fame

When the entire team is nicknamed "the Broad Street Bullies," it means something when you're the biggest bully of them all, as Dave Schultz was for the 1970's Philadelphia Flyers.

Wilson was banned from the PCHA after a vicious stick attack that broke the jaw of Vancouver's Mickey Mackay.

5. SPRAGUE CLEGHORN

Sprague Cleghorn said, "I figure I was in 50 stretcher case fights." The defenseman who played in the NHL from 1918 to 1928 was hockey's equivalent to Ty Cobb. He was one of the best players of his day and one of the most feared, hated by his own teammates. In a 1922 game, Cleghorn injured three of Ottawa's star players. Frank Nighbor suffered a broken arm, Cy Denneny injured his leg, and Eddie Gerard had a head injury, all courtesy of Cleghorn. He did not limit his violence to the ice. Cleghorn was once arrested for beating his wife with a crutch while recovering from a broken leg.

6. JOHN FERGUSON

John Ferguson had the reputation of being one of hockey's best fighters. The left winger played for the Montreal Canadiens from 1963 to 1971. Twelve seconds into his first NHL game, Ferguson got into a fight with Boston's Ted Green. Ferguson broke Bobby Hull's jaw and Ken Schinkel's collarbone. In an American Hockey League game, Ferguson knocked out tough guy Larry Zeidel.

7. BALDY SPITTAL

Baldy Spittal had the reputation of being the dirtiest player of the pre–NHL era. Spittal once split the skull of Cecil Blackford, leaving the Montreal right winger lying in a pool of blood. Spittal was arrested for assault but got away with a $20 fine. In 1904, while playing for Ottawa, Spittal was chased from the arena by fans after slashing an official across the shins during a faceoff.

8. ANDRE DUPONT

Andre Dupont got the nickname Moose because of his mooselike charges. The big defenseman was one of the Philadelphia Flyers' Broad Street Bullies. After a 10-5 victory over Vancouver in February 1973, Dupont said, "It was a good day for us. We didn't go to jail, we beat up their chicken forwards, we scored goals, and we won. Now the Moose drinks beer."

9. LOU FONTINATO

Camille Henry called Lou Fontinato the dirtiest player he had ever seen. Fontinato played for the New York Rangers and Montreal Canadiens from 1954 to 1963. Leapin' Lou had a long and brutal feud with left winger Dirty Bertie Olmstead. In a 1959 game, Fontinato blackened Olmstead's eye, broke his stick over his head, and leaped onto his fallen foe.

10. DALE HUNTER

Left winger Dale Hunter amassed more than 3,500 penalty minutes during his NHL career. In 1993, Hunter was suspended for 21 games for an attack on New York Islanders center Pierre Turgeon. When Turgeon raised his arms to celebrate a goal, Hunter crashed into him, separating his shoulder and causing a concussion.

Good Sports

For every hockey goon there's a gentleman. Toronto Maple Leafs coach Punch Imlach said of his star defenseman, Tim Horton, "Horton's one weakness is that he hasn't a mean bone in his body." Lionel Hitchman, a defenseman who played in the NHL from 1922 to 1934, was so placid that he sometimes apologized after being high sticked, insisting that it was his fault for getting his head in the way. Center Camille Henry accumulated only 88 penalty minutes in 14 NHL seasons. Hall of Fame center Joe Primeau was nicknamed Gentleman because of his kind nature. John Bucyk, the Hall of Fame left wing of the Boston Bruins, won two Lady Byng trophies and had four seasons in which he had spent less than 10 minutes in the penalty box. Alex Delvecchio won three Lady Byng trophies and amassed only 383 penalty minutes in 24 NHL seasons. His career total was less than the number Dave Schultz was penalized in one season.

1. FRANK BOUCHER

Frank Boucher was nicknamed the Gentleman Burglar because of his discrete puck-stealing skills. Between

1922 and 1935, the New York Rangers' center was awarded the Lady Byng Trophy seven times for sportsmanship. In 1935, Boucher was given permanent possession of the trophy. During his 14-year NHL career, Boucher was involved in only one fight.

2. VAL FONTEYNE

Val Fonteyne played left wing for the Detroit Red Wings, New York Rangers, and Pittsburgh Penguins between 1959 and 1972. Fonteyne had five seasons in which he did not receive a single penalty and never had more than four penalty minutes in a season. In 820 NHL games, Fonteyne spent a total of 26 minutes in the penalty box.

3. BILL QUACKENBUSH

Detroit Red Wings All Star defenseman Bill Quackenbush won the Lady Byng trophy in 1949. That season Quackenbush played the entire season without being whistled for a penalty. He played another penalty-free season in 1954.

4. RED KELLY

Red Kelly did not smoke or swear, and rarely drank alcohol. Toronto Maple Leafs scout Squib Walker predicted that the placid Kelly would not last 20 games in the NHL. Instead he played for 20 years. Kelly won the Lady Byng Trophy four times. In the rare instances that he fought, he could more than hold his own. Before he became a professional hockey player, Kelly was a light heavyweight boxing champion in Canada.

5. CLINT SMITH

Clint "Snuffy" Smith was a Hall of Fame center who played for the New York Rangers and Chicago Black

Hawks. Smith won the Lady Byng Trophy in 1939 and again in 1944. During one stretch, he played 85 consecutive games without being called for a penalty.

6. SYL APPS

Toronto Maple Leafs center Syl Apps played the entire 1941–1942 season without receiving a penalty. Not surprisingly, he was awarded the Lady Byng Trophy. Apps was considered a role model because he was a gentleman on and off the ice. In 10 NHL seasons, Apps was penalized only 56 minutes.

7. BILL MOSIENKO

Bill Mosienko had a penalty-free season in 1945 and was awarded the Lady Byng Trophy. The Chicago Black Hawks' right wing also played the entire 1947–1948 season without a penalty.

8. DAVE KEON

Dave Keon, a Hall of Fame center for the Detroit Red Wings, had only 117 penalty minutes during his long NHL career. Keon had four seasons in which he was called for only one 2-minute minor penalty. In 18 NHL seasons, Keon had only one 5-minute major penalty called against him.

9. WAYNE GRETZKY

Wayne Gretzky was not only the greatest player in hockey history, he was also one of the most sportsmanlike. Gretzky won the Lady Byng Trophy in 1980, 1991, 1992, and 1994.

10. MIKE BOSSY

Mike Bossy was another superstar who was rarely penalized. He vowed early in his career not to retaliate.

"Each time you knock me down, I'll get up and score more goals," he said. During his 10-year career with the New York Islanders, Bossy scored 573 goals and had only 210 penalty minutes. The right wing won the Lady Byng Trophy in 1983, 1984, and 1986.

Famous Fights

Barclay Plager said, "It's not how many fights you win, it's how many you show up for." Hockey fights happen almost every game, but some stand out from the rest. In a game during the 1930s, Murray Patrick, who had been the heavyweight boxing champion of the Canadian armed forces, beat Eddie Shore to a pulp. In 1989, Detroit's Joey Kocur broke New York Islanders Brad Dalgarno's eye socket during a fight. On January 4, 1975, Henry Boucha of the Minnesota North Stars fought the Boston Bruins' Dave Forbes. Boucha suffered a 25-inch gash and missed 19 games.

1. PUNCH BROADBENT and AUREL JOLIAT

Punch Broadbent and Aurel Joliat were guests at the 1963 B'nai B'rith banquet in Boston. The Hall of Famers recalled a fight they'd had in a game 40 years previously. Their accounts of the fight differed and the memories rekindled their anger. Broadbent was over 70 years old and Joliat more than 60, but their age did not stop them from renewing their feud. The men exchanged blows and wrestled on the floor.

2.   GORDIE HOWE and LOU FONTINATO

Lou Fontinato had the reputation of being one of hockey's most feared players, but he met his match in a February 1, 1959, game against the Detroit Red Wings. Fontinato took on hockey superstar Gordie Howe. The New York Rangers' defenseman landed three punches before Howe retaliated with crisp combinations. One player described the sound of Howe's punches as like "an axe chopping wood." Fontinato suffered a broken nose.

3.   WAYNE MAKI and TED GREEN

The September, 21, 1969, fight between St. Louis' Wayne Maki and Boston's Ted Green was one of the most brutal in hockey history. Maki speared Green in the abdomen. Green responded by hitting Maki in the shoulder. As Green skated toward the penalty box, Maki hit him over the head with his stick. The force of the blow was so great that skull chips were driven into his brain. Green had five hours of surgery. Maki was suspended for 30 days for his actions.

4.   MARK MESSIER and DENNIS SOBCHUK

Mark Messier scored only one goal with the Cincinnati Stingers of the World Hockey Association during the 1978–1979 season. He caught the eye of Edmonton coach Glen Sather, not because of his play, but because of his fighting ability. Sather witnessed a fight when Messier beat up Oilers center Dennis Sobchuk. When the Edmonton Oilers were incorporated into the NHL, Sather drafted Messier, who developed into one of the league's top scorers.

5. NICK POLANO and GLEN SOMMOR

Most hockey fights are between players, but the principal participants in a bench-clearing brawl between the
Detroit Red Wings and Minnesota North Stars on February 14, 1985, was the team's coaches. Detroit's Nick
Polano and Minnesota's Glen Sommor fought and
wrestled for five minutes. The fight was a standoff and
the game ended in a 5-5 tie.

6. CLARK GILLIES and DAVE SCHULTZ

Philadelphia's Dave Schultz finally met his match in a
1975 Stanley Cup playoff game against the New York
Islanders. In a 1974 Stanley Cup playoff game against
the New York Rangers, Schultz beat up defenseman
Dave Rolfe. A year later Schultz challenged Islanders
rookie left winger Clark Gillies. The 215-pound Gillies
gave Schultz the beating of his life.

7. MAURICE RICHARD and BOB DILL

Bob "Killer" Dill had been banned from the American
Hockey League for rough play. When he arrived in the
NHL with the New York Rangers in 1944, he was intent
on proving his toughness. He called Montreal's Maurice
Richard a "cowardly frog." Richard decked Dill with
one punch. The two continued their battle in the penalty box. Dill suffered a cut over his eye in the exchange.

8. HENRI RICHARD and LEO LABINE

Maurice Richard was not the only member of the family
who could pack a punch. On January 1, 1958, little
brother Henri dropped Boston Bruins tough guy Leo
Labine with a punch that opened an eight-stitch cut. In

the same game, Richard broke the nose of the much bigger Jack Bionda.

9. KENNY REARDON and CAL GARDNER

Montreal's Kenny Reardon and New York's Cal Gardner had a long feud in the late 1940s. In a 1946 game Gardner knocked out six of Reardon's teeth during a fight. On December 31, 1949, Reardon got his revenge by breaking Gardner's jaw. Reardon showed his remorse by saying, "It couldn't happen to a nicer guy."

10. TED LINDSAY and BILL EZINICKI

Detroit's "Terrible" Ted Lindsay and Toronto's "Wild Bill" Ezinicki had a three-minute fight that was one of the most brutal in hockey history. Ezinicki required 19 stitches and had several broken teeth. Lindsay's right hand was so badly injured that he could not close it for 10 days.

Severe Suspensions

Boston's Dave Forbes was suspended for 10 days for hitting Minnesota North Stars Henry Boucha in the face with the butt of his stick. In November 1927, Detroit center Duke Kent was given an indefinite suspension for swinging a stick at a heckling fan in Chicago. In 1913, Joe Hall was suspended for two weeks for hitting referee Tom Melville. All of these players served lengthy suspensions.

1. BILLY COUTU

During the 1927 Stanley Cup playoffs, Boston's Billy Coutu was banned for life from the NHL after smashing referee Gerry LaFlamme in the face. The suspension was lifted five years later, but Coutu never played in the NHL again.

2. BILLY TAYLOR and DON GALLINGER

In 1948, New York center Billy Taylor and Boston center Don Gallinger were expelled from the NHL for gambling on hockey games and knowingly associating with gamblers.

3. **BABE PRATT**

Toronto defenseman Babe Pratt was the NHL's Most Valuable Player in 1944. In 1946, Pratt was suspended for "conduct prejudicial to the welfare of hockey." Pratt had bet on hockey games. Although he could have been banned for life, the suspension was lifted after nine games.

4. **JOE DESSON**

Joe Desson played for the New Haven Blades of the Eastern League. In 1944, he was suspended for life after nearly killing referee Mickey Slowik in a fight.

5. **ART ROSS**

Defenseman Art Ross was one of the best players in the National Hockey Association (NHA). In 1914, Ross asked for a $1,500 salary. Montreal Wanderers owner Sam Lichtenhein imposed a $600 salary cap. Ross declared himself a free agent. In November 1914, the NHA suspended Ross from all organized hockey. A month later the ban was lifted and he joined the Ottawa Senators.

6. **JACK ADAMS**

The Detroit Red Wings won the first three games of the 1942 Stanley Cup finals against the Toronto Maple Leafs. In Game 4, Detroit coach Jack Adams attacked referee Mel Harwood. Adams was suspended for the rest of the playoffs by NHL president Clarence Campbell. Without Adams on the bench, the Red Wings lost four straight games, allowing Toronto to win the Stanley Cup.

7. **ED HOSPODAR**

The Montreal Canadiens have a tradition of shooting the puck into the open net of the opposing team during pregame warm-ups. Prior to Game 6 of the Stanley Cup playoffs against Philadelphia, Montreal's Claude Lemieux slapped the puck into the Flyers' net. Philadelphia defenseman Ed Hospodar took offense and attacked Lemieux, precipitating a 10-minute bench-clearing brawl. Hospodar was suspended for the remainder of the playoffs.

8.   MARTY McSORLEY

In a February 21, 2000, game between Boston and Vancouver, Bruins defenseman Marty McSorley hit Canucks left winger Donald Brashear over the head with his stick. McSorley was suspended for 23 games and Brashear missed six weeks due to the head injury. McSorley was tried for assault because of the attack.

9.   SPRAGUE CLEGHORN

Sprague Cleghorn was too brutal for even his own team. The Montreal Canadiens suspended their star defenseman for the remainder of the 1923 season after a vicious attack on Ottawa defenseman Lionel Hitchman.

10.   JIM SCHOENFELD

In Game 3 of the 1988 Stanley Cup playoff series between New Jersey and Boston, Devils coach Jim Schoenfeld bumped referee Don Koharski. Schoenfeld was suspended by the NHL, but the Devils got a court injunction to allow him to coach Game 4. The regular officials refused to work the game and replacements were used.

Incredible Injuries

N ew York Rangers Red Sullivan suffered a ruptured spleen when he was speared by Montreal's Doug Harvey. On January 29, 2000, Montreal's Trent Mc-Cleary had his larynx crushed when hit by a shot off the stick of Philadelphia's Chris Therien. Just two months later, Toronto's Bryan Berard almost lost his eye after taking a high stick to his face. During the 1947 season, Montreal center Elmer Lach fractured his skull in a game against Detroit. Even spectators can be harmed; 13-year-old Brittanie Cecil died after being struck in the head by an errant puck at a Columbus Blue Jackets game in 2002. Hockey can be a dangerous game.

1. BILL MASTERTON

The only fatality in NHL history took place in a January 13, 1968, game between the Minnesota North Stars and the Oakland Seals. During the first period North Stars center Bill Masterton was sandwiched between the Seals' Larry Cahan and Ron Harris. Masterton flipped backward and hit his head on the ice. He suffered a massive brain injury and died two days later.

2. OWEN McCOURT

On March 6, 1907, Cornwall and Ottawa played a Federal League game. During the game, Cornwall's Owen McCourt was hit in the head by the stick of Ottawa's Charles Masson. McCourt died from the head injury. Masson was tried for manslaughter and acquitted.

3. ACE BAILEY

One of hockey's worst injuries occurred in a December 12, 1933, game between the Boston Bruins and Toronto Maple Leafs. Eddie Shore was tripped by Toronto's King Clancy. Mistaking Ace Bailey for his teammate Clancy, Shore delivered a vicious check from behind. Bailey did a somersault and landed head first on the ice. He fractured his skull and his legs twitched uncontrollably as he lay on the ice. Shore hovered near death for 10 days. A Boston newspaper actually printed his death notice. Bailey's father threatened to kill Shore and had a loaded gun when he was disarmed by the police. Bailey survived, but his hockey career was over.

4. EDDIE SHORE

During his career, Eddie Shore suffered a myriad of injuries. Shore had his nose broken 19 times and had 978 stitches in his face. He fractured his back, hip, and collarbone, and he broke his jaw five times. In 1926, his ear was nearly severed during a fight with Billy Coutu.

5. BERNIE GEOFFRION

In his first NHL game, Bernie "Boom Boom" Geoffrion was checked into the goalpost and broke his nose and had several teeth knocked out. During a practice session on January 28, 1958, Geoffrion suffered a ruptured intestine when he collided with teammate Andre Prevost. Geoffrion was administered his last rites, but he had a full recovery.

6. SHORTY GREEN

Shorty Green played right wing for the New York Americans. He suffered a career-ending injury in a game against the New York Rangers on February 27, 1927. The 150-pound Green was checked hard by 225-pound Rangers defenseman Taffy Abel. Green lost a kidney and never played professional hockey again.

7. CLINT MALARCHUK

Buffalo Sabres goaltender Clint Malarchuk suffered one of the worst injuries in hockey history in a game against the St. Louis Blues on March 22, 1989. Malarchuk collided with Blues winger Steve Tuttle in the goal mouth. Tuttle's skate slashed Malarchuk's neck, severing his jugular vein. The goalie nearly bled to death on the ice before he received medical assistance. The gory sight caused several fans to pass out. Amazingly, Malarchuk spent only one night in the hospital and was back in the Sabres' goal in less than two weeks. He played in the NHL until 1992. As a result of Malarchuk's horrific injury, goaltenders began wearing protective collars to prevent similar injuries.

8. LOU FONTINATO

Lou Fontinato's hockey career came to an end on March 9, 1963, in a game against his old team, the New York Rangers. The Montreal defenseman broke his neck when he and the Rangers' Vic Hadfield crashed into the boards. Fontinato was briefly paralyzed by the neck injury.

9. **IVAN MATULIK**

Ivan Matulik played for the Halifax Citadels of the American Hockey League. During the 1991–1992 season, Matulik had the tip of his nose severed by a skate blade. Players searched for the tip, but could not find it. Later it was found in the icy slush picked up by the Zamboni machine. Doctors were able to successfully attach the nose to Matulik's face.

10. **MARK HOWE**

During a December 27, 1980, game between Hartford and the New York Islanders, Whalers defenseman Mark Howe was impaled on the goal post. Howe suffered a deep laceration of his left thigh.

The Final Horn

Let's end the book with some of hockey's notable lasts.

1. TORONTO ST. PATRICKS and VANCOUVER MILLIONAIRES

The last NHL game in which there were seven players to a side was played on March 2, 1922. The Toronto St. Patricks defeated the Vancouver Millionaires by the score of 6 to 0.

2. JERRY TOPPAZZINI

The last non-goalie to play in the net in an NHL game was Boston Bruins right winger Jerry Toppazini. On October 16, 1960, he replaced injured goaltender Don Simmons in a 5-2 loss to the Chicago Black Hawks.

3. EDDIE JOHNSTON

The last goaltender to play every minute of an entire NHL season was Eddie Johnston. During the 1963–1964 season, Johnston played in all 70 games for the Boston Bruins. Johnston's record for the season was 18-40-12.

4. CHARLIE BURNS

The NHL's last player-coach was Charlie Burns. The center scored three goals for the Minnesota North Stars during the 1969–1970 season. As coach of the North Stars, he was 10-22-12. The next season Burns went back to playing full-time.

5. ANDY BROWN

The last NHL goaltender to play a game without wearing a mask was Detroit's Andy Brown. He last played maskless in a March 31, 1973, game against the St. Louis Blues.

6. BOBBY ORR

Bobby Orr played his last NHL game on November 1, 1978. The incomparable defenseman finished out his career with the Chicago Black Hawks. He was held scoreless in a 1-0 loss to the Vancouver Canucks.

7. GORDIE HOWE

It seemed as though Gordie Howe would play forever. On April 11, 1980, 34 years after his debut, Howe played his last NHL game. The Hartford Whalers' right winger was held scoreless in a 4-3 loss to the Montreal Canadiens.

8. ANDREI KOVALENKO

The Montreal Forum was one of hockey's most storied venues. Montreal right winger Andrei Kovalenko scored the last goal in the Forum on March 11, 1996.

9. CRAIG MacTAVISH

Helmets became mandatory headgear in the NHL in 1979. Any player already in the league was given the option to play without a helmet. The last player to not

London Life-Portnoy/Hockey Hall of Fame

Wayne Gretzky demonstrates some of the magical puck
control that helped him become probably the greatest
hockey player ever, the true "Great One."

wear a helmet was center Craig MacTavish. He retired
in 1997 with 213 goals.

10. **WAYNE GRETZKY**

Wayne Gretzky played his last NHL game on April 18,
1999. The New York Rangers' center had an assist in a
2-1 loss to the Pittsburgh Penguins.

Bibliography

Diamond, Dan. *The Official National Hockey League 75th Anniversary Commemorative Book*. Buffalo: Firefly Books, 1991.

———. *Total Hockey*. Kansas City: Andrews McMeel Publishing, 1998.

———. *Total Stanley Cup*. Toronto: Total Sports, 2000.

Dryden, Steve. *The Hockey News Century of Hockey*. Toronto: McClelland and Stewart, 2000.

———. *The Top 100 NHL Players of All Time*. Toronto: McClelland and Stewart, 1998.

Fischler, Stan, and Shirley Fischler. *The Best, Worst and Most Unusual in Sports*. New York: Fawcett Crest, 1977.

———. *Great Book of Hockey*. Lincolnwood: Publications International, 1996.

Fischler, Stan, Shirley Fischler, Morgan Hughes, Joseph Romain, and James Duplacey. *20th Century Hockey Chronicle*. Lincolnwood: Publications International, 1999.

Hughes, Morgan. *The Best of Hockey*. Lincolnwood: Publications International, 1997.

Liebman, Glenn. *Hockey Shorts*. Chicago: Contemporary Books, 1996.

McFarlane, Brian. *The Best of It Happened in Hockey*. Toronto: Stoddart Publishing, 1998.

Phillips, Louis, and Burnham Holmes. *The Complete Book of Sports Nicknames*. Los Angeles: Renaissance Books, 1994.

Pincus, Arthur. *The Official Illustrated NHL History*. Chicago: Triumph Books, 1999.

Snyder, John. *Hockey!* San Francisco: Chronicle Books, 1994.

Strachan, Al. *One Hundred Years of Hockey*. San Diego: Thunder Bay Press, 1999.

Wallechinsky, David. *The Complete Book of the Olympics*. New York: Penguin Books, 1988.

Weir, Glenn, Jeff Chapman, and Travis Weir. *Ultimate Hockey*. Toronto: Stoddart Publishing, 1999.

Index

About the Author

Floyd Conner is the author of more than a dozen books. His sports books include *Basketball's Most Wanted*, *Golf's Most Wanted*, *Baseball's Most Wanted*, *Day by Day in Cincinnati Bengals History*, and *This Date in Sports History*. He also coauthored *Day by Day in Cincinnati Reds History* and the best-selling *365 Sports Facts a Year Calendar*. He lives in Cincinnati with his wife, Susan, and son, Travis.